Baby and Toddler on Board

Mindful parenting when a new baby joins the family

ORLA KELLY
PUBLISHING

Val Mullally

Orla Kelly Publishing
27 Kilbrody, Mount Oval
Rochestown, Cork,Ireland

Dedicated to my grandchildren.

About The Author

Val Mullally is a Parenting Expert, a Relationship Coach and Founder of Koemba Parenting, who is passionate about supporting parents to create more enjoyable and fulfilling family life. She and her husband have adult children and are grandparents. Val is an experienced teacher and principal and wishes she'd had the opportunity to read this book before her second child was born, especially at that crucial transition time when a new baby joins the family - because she has seen how these insights can support parents to balance the demands of a baby and a toddler, and create environments for these young children to thrive.

Other books by Val:

BEHAVE: What To Do When Your Child Won't - The Three Pointers To Mindful Discipline

Stop Yelling - Nine Steps to Calmer, Happier Parenting

Follow Val Mullally on social media:

Twitter @valmullally https://twitter.com/ValMullally

Pinterest: https://www.pinterest.ie/valmullally

Facebook: https://www.facebook.com/Koemba

YouTube: http://bit.ly/valsyoutube

Contact Val on val@koemba.com

For Val's media kit please see:

https://www.koemba.com/about/media-kit/

Please use this hashtag if you mention this book on social media: #BabyAndToddlerOnBoard

In Praise Of "Baby And Toddler On Board - Mindful Parenting When A New Baby Joins The Family"

"What a delightful and novel way to gently lead parents on their child-rearing journey. Val Mullally shares with us her observations of a toddler making sense of a little sister joining the family. Through her relaxed writing style, she invites the reader along on this journey. I felt I was right with her and her grandson as he jumped into puddles, tumbled off his balance bike, and reacted to disappointment.

You will smile as you see little Liam enjoying his family, and you will enjoy the images of the Danish countryside, parks and homes.

Thank you, Val, for this enlightening book."

Patricia K. Martin PhD Clinical Psychologist

"I have found reading this book very helpful as a grandmother of a three year old toddler with her 8 month brother.

It has been most interesting to read … an opportunity to share in an experience I can relate to and learn, without realising I am learning skills to apply in my interaction with children. I also regularly look after two little brothers, one of whom has

Down's syndrome/additional needs and the principles in Val's book apply every bit as much with children with special needs. I found the book quick and easy to read and I enjoyed observing the journey the author was on and learning from her experience.

It is an excellent book in understanding children and relating to them meaningfully in our ever-changing society, whether they are your own children, grandchildren or foster children."

Sharon Yarr

"This is an essential and enlightening read for anyone who wants to create a calm and loving home where there is mutual respect and contentment. Val's practical, insightful examples and experiments really encourage mindful and fulfilling parenting. The easy-to-read style and helpful tips make it a book that you will want to pick up for reference again and again. Reading this book will be one of the most beneficial things you can do in preparing for, or coping with, a new addition to the family."

Jennifer McKeague (mum of two lively and lovable boys)

"I absolutely love this book. I am not a native English speaker, but I had no problems to understand. It's well written, easy to read and follow and I couldn't put it down. So many interesting points covered. I read a lot of parenting books already, but this one gave me a new insights and showed me where I could improve to help my little ones become more confident and happy.

I enjoyed the stories and examples and learnt from them how to deal with my own situations.

I already put it into test with my two toddlers (2 and 3 years olds). I still have a few things to do to create better environment for all of us, but parenting is a journey and this book is a great tool to help you get where you want to be. Mindful parent with happy kids and calmer home."

Pavla Jurasek (mother of two young children)

I love this book! I absolutely love it!

I often say that reading " The Womanly Art of Breastfeeding" is like reading a hug. With this book, it's like "chatting over a cuppa". The style is so relaxed and informal. I feel like I'm sitting with a trusted friend, who isn't trying to tell me how or what to do with my parenting, but rather someone who is genuinely invested in my home being a happy one.

The introduction is gorgeous. It's so wonderful how the author immediately relates both her desire to connect with her grandson, but also his need for respectful space. I also love how honest Val Mullally is about her own parenting experiences in the past, and how that is what has led her on this path and to this approach to parenting. This makes everything so much more relatable for the parents reading this book.

Val gives gentle, thoughtful and compassionate suggestions on meltdowns and toddlers being stubborn. There are also really useful, practical and easy-to-do tips on toddler tantrums, and other challenges that parents often face at this stage.

As a reader, you can feel the empathy for toddler Liam and how important it is that he's given the vocabulary to help him deal with his experiences, to make sense of it; and that he is given the space and respect to feel the range of emotion.

The book also discusses, "How safe is safe enough?" This is the question we all ask ourselves with toddlers. We want them to be fearless explorers, to trust their own judgement, to trust their bodies and movements and decisions - but where to draw the line between fearless explorer and child needing safety restrictions. I think this is handled really well by the author, both in this part of the book and also in the Setting Limits chapter. She also discusses the important topic of containing our own anxiety.

Val's downloadable tips are handy to stick on the fridge or kitchen press. Having them in the book is wonderful but because the majority of our time together is spent in the kitchen, whether eating, playing, drawing etc. That's where conflict / challenging behaviour would usually arise. Sneaking a quick peek at the fridge door can make the difference between toddler (and parent!) meltdown, and toddler meltdown diffusing quickly with a patient and in-touch parent.

Also it's lovely that she acknowledges that parenting a baby and a toddler isn't easy; she makes that ok for the parents too. This book is not overwhelming, it's not too wordy, it's not preachy - simple, manageable and bite-size, which is pretty much all a parent with a toddler and new-born can, or wants, to handle.

This book is sweet, simple, succinct, easy-to read, and non-judgemental. Lovely!

Caz Koopman Founder of Gentle Discipline (Ireland)

You can follow new updates and discussion about this book by using the hashtag #BabyAndToddlerOnBoard

For more information visit:

https://www.koemba.com/baby-and-toddler-on-board-book/

Foreword

I wish I had Val's book when I was parenting my toddler and baby as there were plenty of times when I got frustrated and didn't understand how best to handle the situation.

In my experience, now that they have grown up a bit (and how quickly they grow!), toddler-time and teenage-hood seem to be the two trickiest times because reason doesn't always work and these are both very emotional times for children as they grow and change so rapidly at these points.

Val's book uses a story-based approach; stories that will resonate and completely make sense, as she explores how parenting is done in Denmark, where her grandchildren live. I found it really interesting learning about how Danish parents approach parenting. It makes you realise how much parents in UK, Ireland and USA, have become helicopter parents, hovering over their kids, afraid to let them take calculated risks, worried about them constantly. Val's book teaches us that children learn through their experiences, and allowing them to have those experiences (in a safe way of course!) definitely makes for emotionally healthier and more resilient kids.

This book also gives parents practical tips to implement around different scenarios. Little steps you can take or changes you can make to parent your toddler in a more relaxing way for both you and your child.

This is a warm, caring parenting book, one you will hug to yourself as you read!

Jill Holtz, (mum of 2 and co-founder of <u>MyKidsTime. com)</u>.

Resources for Readers

Dear Reader,

To accompany this book, I have prepared complementary resources to support you on your parenting journey as you adapt to the challenges of a baby and a toddler on board. It's not always easy to be the parent you want to be, especially when you have to meet the parenting demands of two little people with different needs, different personalities, abilities and different timetables. Here are helpful insights and practical tips, devised to help you take care of yourself and your little ones during this time of adjustment to being a larger family.

Download your "Carer's Checklist for Minding a Toddler": a practical resource you can use to prepare for when you may need to call on someone for support at the time of your baby joining your family: https://www.koemba.com/baby-and-toddler-resources/

You will also be able to access various new resources as we post them on the Koemba Parenting website. These resources are my gift to you to support you in your parenting journey.

This "Baby and Toddler On Board" book will help if you:

- are concerned that you may become stressed or overwhelmed with the challenges of parenting two, or more, young children

- want to help your toddler feel included and accepting of your second child

- want to know how to best deal with discipline issues with your toddler during this transition in the family

- want to build connection with your baby from the earliest days

- want to ensure that your toddler still feels your love and keeps in close connection with you

- want to know how to help your children to grow towards their full potential

- This book is also helpful for the grandparent, spouse or friend wanting tips and insights on how best to support the mother and the family on the arrival of a second child.

Here's to your home being one of joy, exploration, discovery and connection for all of you!

#BabyAndToddlerOnBoard

Val Mullally

CONTENTS

Introduction

You've probably picked up this book because you're facing the challenge of how to cope with a toddler on the arrival, or pending arrival, of a baby in the home.

- If you are looking for guidelines and practical tips on how to create a happy home for your children, and for yourselves, here's help.

- If you are in a support role to a young family, this book is also for you.

It has taken me raising two sons, over quarter of a century's teaching experience, and years of further training in childcare, holistic development, relationship theory, life coaching, interpersonal communications, and neurolinguistic programming, plus reading a mountain of books, to reach the stage where I term myself Parenting Expert.

The teachers and guides in one of the most informative parts of my lifelong path of education are my grandchildren. I'm inviting you to share a grandmother's personal journey - the ups and downs of the parenting roller coaster when the family welcome a second child into the home.

Whilst this book happens to be set in the home of a heterosexual couple, the principles of this book can be applied to any type of family raising a toddler, or pre-schooler, and a baby.

There will of course still be unexpected dips and bends in the road of your parenting journey, bumpy patches, and fabulous, unexpected joys. This book offers you a map to guide you through these experiences.

Are you are asking yourself,

"How will I manage the needs of a toddler AND a newborn?"

In this book you'll discover three key insights to help you create a more harmonious home. You'll discover how to interact with the toddler, or preschooler, in a way that will support their needs during this time of change in family life, with a chapter at the end of each section relating to baby's needs too.

Ideally read this book before baby arrives, to equip you in setting the groundwork with yourself and your toddler, and your support team, ahead of time.

Let's join a grandmother on her journey with her toddler grandson as the birth of his sister approaches, to discover how to create an easier and happier transition when you welcome baby into your home.

The Journey Begins - How to Connect With a Toddler

I kiss my husband. I'm not doing a good job at holding back the tears. It's hard to say goodbye. We will be apart for a month. Our son and daughter-in-law have asked me to stay with them in Denmark. The baby is due any day now. They've asked me to be on "toddler duty". As the plane steers us through the clouds, away from Dublin, I flick through the pages of the in-flight magazine but my thoughts dance around the weeks ahead. How do I be the grandmother I want to be? I'm a fairly young "far-mor" (the Danish word for paternal grandmother) but do I have the stamina to keep up with my grandson's energy level? Liam is a twenty-three month old Viking — big, blond and strong, with an adventurous spirit.

How can I support the family so the arrival of a sibling will be a happy memory for my toddler grandson?

How can I assist in creating a foundation for happy relationships as the siblings get older?

My career has focused on working with children and parents - but will my parenting approach be what's needed when I'm immersed in the world of toddler-dom?

Will my theories work for my own family?

The plane taxis into Copenhagen Airport ahead of schedule. Soon my suitcase lurches onto the conveyor belt. It's good to feel the warmth of the afternoon sunshine as I wait in the pick-up zone outside the terminal. My son's little black car eases into sight. The family clamber out the car to greet me. My son, Alwyn, bends to kiss me. Sophia kisses and hugs me, her protruding belly reminding me that their family will soon be four.

"Farmor!" exclaims my grandson. It's great to hear him call me by name.

As we drive home I'm on the back seat next to him. It's been three months since he has last seen me. That's a long time from a toddler's perspective. I know I must connect on his terms — he's strapped into his car-seat which means he can't retreat. I need to take it slow so he can feel comfortable with me again.

"Hi, Liam!" I smile and make eye contact, but I keep well over to my side of the car so I don't encroach his space. He gives a quick smile, then breaks eye contact. I wait. I don't hurry to establish the contact. He stares ahead at the road for a while. I let him set the pace.

He glances at me. I glance back with a slight smile. But I don't try to hold his gaze. I follow his lead.

Then "Lello" he informs me. He has a yellow toy car in his hand.

I look at the toy car he's holding,

"Yellow. A yellow car. You've got a yellow car."

His chubby toddler arm reaches out towards me, so I can see his car. Contact established!

I am thankful for the parenting insight and skills I can use to establish a harmonious connection, where the interaction flows between us. Join me on this journey of a month with a toddler to discover my experience of what helped, and what didn't, in making the arrival of a sibling a smooth transition for the family, and especially for the toddler. You will find three sections in this book that explore the three key insights every parent can use:

1. Follow the Child's Lead

2. Cross the Bridge

3. Hearth Your Home

I wish I had been aware of this approach to parenting when my kids were young. I thought it was my job to make my kids "behave". *I'm the parent. I'm supposed to be in charge, aren't I? My kid needs to learn to behave!* I was an experienced teacher. I thought I knew how to parent. But by the time my second son got to his teens, it was clear my child needed something different and so did I. "Show your child who is boss" - expecting a child to do what they were told - was causing us all heartache.

The crisis in our relationship forced me to take a long and careful look at what it means to be a parent and what children need to thrive. Fast forward the clock to the present day — I now have more than twenty years of research into what creates healthy family relationships I'm thankful for the privilege of my adult children and their families in my life. Now I have the amazing experience of revisiting the world of parenting a toddler, with my grandson. Here's what I discovered.

SECTION A

FOLLOW THE CHILD'S LEAD

To lead the people, walk behind them.
Lao-Tzu

1.

Follow Your Child's Lead - Introduction

Life would be so much simpler if your toddler flowed with you and your agenda! But that is not the reality of any parent living in toddler-dom, especially when a baby is welcomed into the home. In this first part of the journey, we will share different ways in which to follow your toddler's lead, and why this approach matters.

The term "follow the child's lead" is often used in Early Education. Effective educators know the power of following the child's lead - to start where the child is at. But they also are aware of what "follow the child's lead" is not. Follow the child's lead is not allowing the child to do whatever they please. It is not leaving the child without structure and support. It is an environment with boundaries to ensure safety and respect for child and adult alike, which gives the child the space, safety and support to discover the wonderful and complex world in which they live.

Together we'll explore how to follow a child's lead in different everyday experiences:

- in simple interactions
- in art activities
- in play

- in supporting the child to risk "failure"
- in what matters to the child

We will take a peek at the everyday experiences of following the lead with a toddler. We'll discuss the challenges you might face as you follow your child's lead, as you create a home where you can all thrive.

Let's begin as I share the secrets I've learned about how to make meaningful connection, even when a toddler is feeling shy.

2.

What To Do When A Child Feels Shy

Have you ever watched a well-meaning adult trying to "make friends" with your child - but your child goes into *head down, stare at the floor, hide behind parent, won't talk* mode? It's hard as a parent when there's someone you care about who wants to connect with your child - but your child doesn't want to engage.

Your parent or your best friend comes to visit. "Hello Johnny!" they exclaim. Maybe they try to kiss him or pick him up. Johnny disappears behind your jeans, clinging so tightly you hope your jeans don't part company with your hips.

"Oh Johnny, you're such a big boy now, let me look at you!"

The more the well-intended adult tries to connect, the more determined your toddler is to stay out of sight. This isn't going how you had hoped.

Here is the little known path to build connection when a child feels shy. What is this path? Rapport. Conscious awareness of building rapport happens when we move our focus from our own agenda to seeing life through the eyes of the child. This is vital when we want to deepen our relationship with the child.

What is rapport?

Rapport is a natural connection - the soft gaze, comfortable body contact, sense of ease, relaxed tone of voice, a relaxed to-and-fro between the two. When you see a couple in love, the rapport is so obvious it could be a flashing neon sign. We can sense the rapport in a relationship we're observing, even when we can't hear what is being spoken. And the often unknown part of that path is the knowledge that you can consciously build rapport to create a better, smoother relationship with your child. But the art of rapport-building has often had bad press: think of the smooth-talking salesman who's acting as though he is your buddy. *He's trying to coerce me.* We intuitively sense the lack of sincere positive intention, the feigned connection, the falsity which destroys meaningful interaction.

But that sales-pitch scenario is so different from genuine rapport. In fact, it undermines it because rapport is always about being there for the other. Think about that couple in love. When they are in rapport, each wants to please the other. You forget about your own desires and your own agenda and instead you are immersed in the other's experience.

How to build rapport with a toddler

When you want to build rapport with a toddler it starts from the basis of respect - the toddler is their own person. You take the child's perspective into account. If you want to develop this secret path to connection then don't barge into the relationship. Your big smiling hello could undermine the rapport you want to create. Be sensitive to the child's needs, their timing and their interests. This is "following the child's lead" - as I did when Liam showed me his yellow car. I pace myself to his timing — I wait until he is ready to connect. I follow what interests him. I'm aware of his energy level and I attune myself to his wavelength. I may be bubbling with excitement to see the ones I love, but if I want to connect with the child, I need to "park" my own emotional state and tune in to his. If he is slow and hesitant coming forward, I slow and wait until he is ready to connect. I smile a quick smile, or say a few words, but then I wait for his response. It's a beautiful and sensitive dance between us. I follow his lead. He responds. I respond.

So here are the stepping-stones on the rapport path that can move your relationship from disconnect to "I get you and we are in this together." Rapport is about a cosy sameness — I'm in tune with him and I'm interested in what interests him. We both admire the yellow car. When you establish this sense of sameness, you establish the connection. It's a "dance" between the two of you with the same tone of voice, the same strength of voice and the same gestures. You smile - I smile. You look at me, I look at you. You glance away, I glance away too. You look back at me, I look back at you. We share the same angling of the head, the same eye connection.

We echo the same sound effects: when he "brmms" the car across the seat, I "brmm" my hand along my side of the car at the same speed and in the same direction.

Try mirroring your toddler at times when you want to connect. Follow their lead and watch them respond!

But, as parents, don't we already have a connection with our children?

Rapport is not a given; it is not a stable, fixed state. We fall in and out of connected relationship. In the film "As Good As It Gets", Melvin (Jack Nicholson) takes Caroline (Helen Hunt) out for a meal to a fancy restaurant. They chat and laugh, they gaze warmly at each other, and their body movements mirror one another, in an enchanting dance. The evening goes fabulously until he complains to her that he doesn't know why he is expected to wear a jacket yet she is allowed into the fancy restaurant in an ordinary day dress. The rapport is gone - and so is she! Watch this part of the movie with the sound muted to see the couple go from warm rapport to instant disconnect. When he comments on her plain dress she takes it as an insult — it slams a wedge between them.

We don't deliberately break connection with our children but, like the film character Melvin, we don't always get the other person's take on a situation. We miss something important to the other. Our own thoughts and emotions crowd our minds. Suddenly - disconnect! At times our rapport is strong, and at other times connection plummets. Rapport is not a constant.

The good news is, when we are aware, we can consciously create rapport. We can repair a rupture in the relationship. When we sense things are off-kilter, we can use rapport-building skills to re-establish connection — to recreate the comfortable interaction with our child. To build rapport follow the child's lead and the child's pace.

So what to do when an adult isn't tuned in to your child?

If you face a situation where an adult isn't sensitive to your child's initial experience, make a response that will downplay the scenario, rather than exacerbate it. If you make a comment, like, "She's shy!" you are stating that is a characteristic of the child. Your child is then more likely to take on that personality type. Rather comment about this as an emotion or behaviour:

"She's feeling shy right now," or "She's acting shy - she'll soon settle in."

If you keep a calm, low-key response it makes it easier for the child to assess the situation and choose to interact when they are ready. It can be challenging when an adult isn't sensitive to your child, but recognise your child needs you to be their gate-keeper in a situation like this. If your child wants to hide behind you, let them do so. That's their safe place right now, when they feel insecure because this is a person they don't know, or one they haven't seen for a while; or your child may feel threatened by an over-friendly adult who perhaps isn't sensitive to their needs. This can happen with loving relatives who forget the child doesn't know them yet, or might feel uncertain after time apart, even though there is a strong family bond. If the spotlight is kept on the child - "Now say hello" - they are likely to become more introverted. Take the focus off your child by chatting with the visitor about other things, keeping a gentle body contact with your child if possible. Once the child feels safe they will begin to "reappear" and, when they sense a connection with the adult, they will start interacting. If the adult is someone who will be in your child's life, perhaps you can encourage them to read these first four chapters ahead of the first meeting and reflect on these rapport-building principles, where they can see how I connected with my toddler grandson after several months apart. See especially the next chapter on how to connect with a toddler.

But why does rapport matter in parenting?

Rapport matters because when your child experiences you are in tune with them, they will want to connect. When your child senses you are in flow with them, they will feel comfortable, and when they feel safe, they will respond. The more the trust builds between the two of you, the more you will get to see and enjoy your toddler's "real me".

Here is your chance to peep over my shoulder and see how to follow the child's lead in the small, everyday interactions.

3.

Practical Tips to Connect with a Toddler

If there's a well-meaning adult who has been out of the picture and who you know wants to connect with your child, ask them to read this page! Rather than trying to manoeuvre your child to "Say hello nicely", it is the adult's responsibility to connect with the child in a way that makes it safe enough for the child to want to engage. Relationships need to unfold in their own time and in their own way.

Five Keys to Create Rapport With A Child

1. Be mindful

Be aware of your own emotional state. Be aware of your child's.

Anxiety, or over-excitement, can create awkward reactions. Temper your own emotional reaction to whatever situation is unfolding. Listen and observe so you can tune in to the child's emotions.

2. Tune in to your child's energy

If the child is excited and bouncy, raise your energy level of excited and bouncy to match theirs — unless you are trying to settle them! If the child is quiet and reserved, and you are excited, draw in your own energy to level with them.

3. Be aware of the child's eye contact

If the child is not making eye contact, give only a quick glance. When they break eye contact, don't "pursue" with your gaze. Rather, look away as well, and observe the child out of the corner of your eye. When you sense them "coming back" be there to meet them with your eyes.

4. Practise the art of "soft gaze"

This is the opposite of a hard stare - look at the difference in the mirror. Consciously let the area around your eyes soften. Consciously choose "soft gaze" rather than an intent stare, when you are trying to establish contact with a young child.

5. Follow the child's lead

Match the child's eye contact, expressions, energy, movements, tone and interests. To reflect on this, you might choose to reread the introductory chapter about my first face-to-face interaction for several months with Liam in "The Journey Begins - How to Connect With a Toddler".

We have begun following the child's lead. Now let's discover how this can be helpful in the different situations parents, grandparents and caregivers encounter!

4

How to Strengthen Your Relationship with Your Toddler

Liam's plump little fingers take my hand and he leads me into the garden. *He's choosing to connect.* We have now moved from a tentative rapport to him experiencing me as safe.

"Sit," he tells me. I plonk myself on a low, three-legged stool.

He picks up a short piece of chalk lying between the pebbles. He draws a few marks on the concrete beneath my feet.

"You're drawing a line. And another line." I use my comments to follow his action.

He passes me the chalk. I draw a few lines, copying the marks he has made, and then I give the chalk to him. The dance of rapport!

He adds a few lines and hands the diminishing piece of chalk to me.

The chalk is handed back and forth between us as we take turns drawing marks on the concrete; each time I follow his lead of what to draw, until the chalk becomes too short to use.

I don't make my own picture and draw his attention to it. I don't say, "That's beautiful", because I would detract him from his own creation. I would take his attention to my assessment of his work. I keep my attention on what has his attention. When I comment, "You're drawing a line. And another line," this is far more affirming for him than saying, "What a beautiful picture" because I am keeping my attention where he has his attention. I am staying present to his world and to his experience. I follow his pace and I follow his agenda of what he wants to do. It's easy to do this if I follow his gaze, and notice the direction he is headed, physically and mentally.

The more child-friendly a garden is, the greater will be the opportunities to connect. Develop your powers of observation to notice what has caught your child's attention. Whether your toddler is pushing a toy car, watching an ant, reading a book, digging in the sand - in each situation there is the potential to follow the child's lead and build rapport.

Liam rises off his haunches and points to the greenhouse.

"'Matoes" he says. We are off in search of ripe tomatoes.

5.

Why Toddler Scribbles Aren't Scribbles

Before Liam and I wander into the greenhouse, let's take a time to reflect on a particular situation as an example of how to follow the child's lead. Let's discuss drawing.

How a toddler learns to draw

It's easy to draw for your child - a sun, a person, a tree. Maybe there is a time when your child *wants* you to draw but if you are drawing they aren't. Your child does not learn to draw by watching you draw. They learn to draw by drawing.

Your toddler pushes a bright coloured stick on the paper and it makes a mark; a learning experience in itself. We as adults see random lines the child has made. We see mindless marks on a piece of paper. But a toddler scribbling is not "scribbling" as we adults understand it. For the toddler, it's a mindful activity.

Your toddler discovers they can make marks on the paper. They can put more colour. They can use different colours. They can make marks all over the paper. They discover the red crayon always makes a red line and the yellow crayon always makes a yellow line. They discover they can draw longer lines and shorter lines. They can press hard and make a dark line. Or when they press lightly the mark is hardly there at all. They can make different type of marks. Little dots. Long lines. Wavy lines. Lines crossing each other. This is not mindless scribbling. This is discovery. And it is part of their development, for which they need time and repeated experience to absorb. They are developing muscle control, eye-hand coordination and observation skills.

Stages of drawing

Scribbling is the foundation stage of meaningful drawing. Over time, they learn how to draw in a circular motion. They learn how to make different combinations of lines and they will tell you, "Dog", "Sun" or whatever they draw — though it looks like scribbles to you. Then they begin to connect their lines. A circle with wobbly lines radiating out from it. The sun.

Daddy. At first they draw a "potato man" with eyes and mouth on the centre of a circle, and arms and legs extending directly from this central shape. Then, over the months, they learn how to draw a separate body and head. They are observing and they're learning how to record what they're observing.

Their drawings become recognisable. A dog begins to look like a dog. A tree looks like a tree. They learn to connect straight lines to draw shapes like houses. They begin to create pictures with different things in the picture and to position things where they need to be. The sun is at the top of the paper, in the sky. The house is on the ground at the bottom. We sometimes overlook these important stages of their drawing development. As adults we forget this is a huge learning process.

The child needs plenty of opportunity to observe and to explore drawing. They need to create, without an adult imposing their idea of what a tree or a dog or a man should look like. The toddler needs creative space without others interrupting with their ideas.

How to follow your child's lead in drawing

If they want you to draw too, follow the child's lead. If they draw two quick little lines, you draw two quick little lines, in your own drawing space - not interfering with their working space, unless they indicate they want you to. If they want you involved, then let your drawing reflect what they are drawing. If you start drawing your own stuff, you're not accompanying them on their discovery. You are off on a different journey and they might lose focus on what had their attention.

Of course, it's great for children to see grown-ups doing their own artwork too. But when you accompany the child in their drawing experience, don't distract them. Follow the child's lead.

And we can follow the child's lead in so many other situations as well.

6.

How to Approach Potty Time

Until recent years I did not understand that even with toileting, we can follow the child's lead, rather than impose without being aware of how this is for the child.

"Let's change your diaper," Sophia says to Liam.

(Sophia has spent time abroad, and she uses the term "diaper", so I consciously choose the word that is familiar to my grandson).

I need to be clear about toilet routine, so I can be sensitive to Liam's needs. I've raised my own sons, so I know *what* to do, but I need to know *how* to do.

Some details can be described in a caregiver's checklist but the intimate moments in relationship, when a child could feel vulnerable or defensive, can only be understood by observing.

I need to know their normal routine so Liam will feel safe and comfortable when I need to help him with his nappy-changing. When we create cooperation in toileting, we don't undermine the child's sense of self; the child doesn't need to feel out of control concerning the most personal aspects of the body. This is a time where a sense of connection and treating the other with gentle respect is as important as if you were helping a frail adult with their ablutions.

Liam walks with his Mama to the bathroom. I ask if I can come too.

"Shall we take your diaper off." Sophia's voice and movements are calm. She's respectful of Liam as a person.

He pulls down his diaper and Mama helps. They cooperate with one another. Everything goes smoothly.

"Bye bye, pooh." He presses the button for the toilet to flush.

Together Sophia and Liam wash their hands. Toileting is not done "to" him. It is a routine they share together.

I ask Liam if I can fasten his new diaper. He looks at me; a slight furrow on his brow. *This is something Mama or Papa do!* But he stands still to let me position the fresh diaper and secure the tapes.

Little steps like this are going to make it easier for us both when I take on the role of caregiver especially with a child who has a strong Viking spirit!

7.

How to Support an Adventurous Toddler

We're at the playground. Liam is in his element. There are irregularly-placed knobs on the sloped wall to climb to the slide. This is a challenge for a toddler, but soon he is at the top. It's not a huge slide - it is about six feet off the ground, but that is pretty big when you are three feet tall.

He slides down.

Then he runs to the climbing wall to begin again.

He slides down a few times, then he notices an older child run up the slide. He wants to do that too. He soon gets the hang of it. He clambers to the top, then he slides down on his tummy, feet first.

"Fun," he says. "Happy!"

Sophia follows his lead, trusting him to explore. Where he is confident in his capabilities, she keeps low profile. When he looks towards her, he sees her relaxed smile and warm gaze.

Observing an anxious mother

Imagine a different scenario. As soon as a child puts her hands on the first rung of the ladder, her mother lifts her to the top of the climbing frame. The child takes small, careful steps along the platform — she sits on the top of the slide and her tiny body tenses. Her hands grip the sides of the slide and she stares blankly, her facial expression frozen. Her mother lifts out her arms towards her.

"Come on, darling," she coaxes her child to let go her grip on the rails. She catches her child into her arms when she's slid only halfway down. Here's a loving, attentive parent, yet this over-protectiveness isn't helpful. When your child senses your worry whenever she attempts something, the message your child hears is:

"You aren't able to do this by yourself."

How to develop your child's confidence

When your child attempts a new challenge, at first stay close enough at hand, in case your child gets into difficulty. Quietly observe. Your body language needs to give the message you believe in their competence. Give them the opportunity to test their own abilities. Only help if your child needs help. Don't move in unless necessary; which means you need to contain your own anxiety. Anxiety is a highly contagious emotion. Focus on your breathing and choose calm. Once your toddler has mastered the skill, move further away, so they can play without you in their space — unless they want you right there!

When you give your child the message - non-verbal as well as verbal - that you trust them to be able do a task or take on a challenge - they develop confidence in their own competence. They learn to trust themselves.

You may be wondering about your responsibility to keep your child safe. We will get to that later.

A few days later I learn another lesson in following a toddler's lead...

8.

How to Tune In To Your Child's Experience - "Fire Enja!"

It's Saturday morning and Alwyn is home today. An outing is a great idea and together we discover a fleamarket with artisan breads, home-made preserves, bright-coloured clothes swinging on hangers and cartons of bric-a-brac. Some stalls sell second-hand toys; it's a good opportunity to buy a gift for Liam. I spot a large yellow dumper truck. *He'll like that.*

Liam and his Papa perch on a large low rock, surveying the market activity.

"Come, Liam. Come see what I found."

I take his hand and we walk to the stall. I lift the tipper truck into his hands. He gives it a long considered look then places it back on the table. *I thought he would love it!* He stares at the far end of the table.

He points. "Fire enja!"

The gleaming red vehicle is about a foot long. This is not a toy intended for a toddler but for a six-year-old - or even an eight-year-old. Liam keeps pointing at the fire engine. His gaze doesn't shift. Nothing else on the table exists. He wants the fire engine. The stall-keeper lifts it and passes it to us. It is a beautiful vehicle. It has intricate details - perfect little wheels, extendable ladder, fire hoses, blue lights. It is well made - but it's too intricate to withstand the robust treatment of a toddler.

"Wow, a big red fire-engine!"

He keeps examining it. I try to distract. "Liam, shall we look and see what other toys are here?" His gaze is fixed on the red beauty. This is not a distractable moment. It is not a persuadable moment. This is "fire enja" or meltdown. His heart is set on it.

I weigh up the situation. *Why not let him choose!* I calculate the cost - about six euro. Reasonable price. Maybe it will get broken in a few days, but there is six euro worth of enjoyment here.

"You want the fire-engine?" I don't know why I'm asking. It's evident. I pay the stall-keeper and we return to Papa.

"Fire enja!" Liam exclaims, holding the shiny vehicle for his father to admire. The two of them begin the inspection, sliding the ladder to its full height above Liam's head, opening the side-lockers and examining the tiny axes, spades and hoses set into the interior.

I leave him and Papa exploring the intricacies of the toy engine and I wander to a nearby stall. I am eyeing the cluttered display of jewelry when I hear the sound of a siren. At first I think it's the sound of a distant emergency vehicle. I turn around. Liam is jumping up and down; his hands clenched in little fists of joy and his eyes glowing. On the ground the little engine flashes its blue light, its siren blaring.

"Ba-boo, ba-boo, ba-boo!"

They've discovered the operating switch!

This truck is his treasure.

I'm glad I followed his lead. He knew. I had underestimated his competence. He is a unique person with his own interests, likes and dislikes. I'm not saying to buy everything a child demands, but observe your child's reaction. What captures your child's interest?

Today, because I followed his lead rather than imposing my idea of what he'd like, he guided me to what matters to him and I learnt more of who this child uniquely is.

I soon discover each day holds new insights on how to follow a toddler's lead.

9

What To Do When A Toddler Faces a Big Challenge

Over the weekend we take an outing to the plant nursery. Alwyn and Sophia want an ornamental tree for the garden. I take toddler-duty so they can stroll round together and look at their options.

Liam sets off on the downhill path through the jungle of plants. He turns the corner into a broader path. There in the clearing stands a huge, gleaming tractor towering above him. The awesomeness of it lights up his eyes. It's stationary. Silent. No-one is around.

Liam, the intrepid explorer, moves closer to inspect. I'm behind him. I'm observing. I'm assessing. But I say nothing. Right now his world is this magnificent machine. My comment is not needed.

He smoothes his hand over the gleaming blue paint. The black rubber of the front wheel arches above his head. His eyes set on the metal rungs to climb to the cab. He reaches for the lowest bar and hoists himself upward. His foot finds the lowest rung. He clambers onto the first step. A huge step. It's designed for an adult man, not for a toddler. The second rung. Up he pulls himself until he can reach the door of the cab. He tugs the handle but the door won't open.

"Kukoo," he says. (Toddlerese for "Broken.")

"It's locked." I say. I focus on where his attention is and give him words to describe why he can't open it.

He stands there for a moment. Taking it all in from the highest step alongside the cab. Then he decides to clamber down. His leg reaches down, down. Searching for a foothold below him that he can't see. His hands cling the rung above him, as his body stretches, stretches downwards. His arms strain with his body weight. He can't find a foothold. His brow furrows and his mouth opens. He needs help.

I use my hand and relocate his foot on the rung where he had been before. I assess. His hand is too high on the bar above. He needs to lower his grip so he can lower his body enough for his foot to connect with the rung below - the rung he was groping to find. I don't lift him down. I believe he's capable. But he needs help in figuring out how to do this. I am close enough to catch him if needed.

"Liam, you need to bring your hand down first." I stretch up. I help him relocate his hand to a lower position. Now his hand is lower, he can move his leg to a lower position. His foot can engage the rung beneath him. He moves to the next rung.

"Now bring your hand down again." By the final rung he has it figured, without me saying anything.

He was already capable, but he needed guidance to develop his competence in a new climbing situation.

Keeping a toddler safe

I imagine you might be reading this and thinking,

"My job is to keep my child safe!"

Of course your job is to keep your child safe. I agree. When you support your naturally capable child to develop his competence you also help him to learn how to keep himself safe. If Liam were ever in a similar climbing situation again, where he can't find his foothold, he will know to reposition his handhold to give himself more leverage. He will integrate this newly learned competency into his repertoire of "this is how I climb down" skills and he will apply it to other similar situations. Yes, he will need a few more practice rounds to get the hang of it. If I stopped him from climbing, or if I lifted him down, I would have given him the message:,

"You are not able to do this." I would have eroded his confidence.

He might have slipped and had a bruise or a few scrapes but he's not climbing the Eiffel Tower. This challenge is within his capability.

If he were to face a similar situation in later years, but he hadn't learnt the skills he needs, he would be unlikely to attempt a new feat — mortifying for a teenager with his peers. Or he could be seized with anxiety, which will stop him figuring out what is needed, and risk a bad fall. A child's exploration is key preparation for the challenges of life. Alternatively, if I had not been close enough to support Liam, he could have panicked when he couldn't find a foothold. The distress could erode his confidence. By supporting him to develop his competence - his ability to figure things out - I increase his confidence. Successful people take risks with confidence because they have developed the brain circuitry and skills to assess situations and take the steps needed to navigate the challenges.

Living in rural Ireland, I know there is always concern around the potential dangers of farm machinery. I raised my sons in the unforgiving African terrain of poisonous spiders, snakes, scorpions and centipedes, not to mention the larger beasts. What I discovered is we don't keep our children safe by bubble-wrapping them because sooner or later they will either emotionally suffocate and lose confidence in their ability, or they will rebel against our efforts and venture into the big, wide world without the self-awareness and skills they need. The unprepared child, who has not been allowed to develop their competency through exploration, is most in danger of getting hurt.

Developing your toddler's competence

Believe your child is capable. Give opportunities - and unobtrusive help if needed - to develop their competence. When you support your child to develop their competence, you support them to confidently handle life. Follow what interests them. Follow their developing physical, cognitive and spiritual capabilities. The confident child grows to be a confident adult; one who takes on the challenges of life because they know they are able, or confident they can figure out how.

Does the exploring child experience failure? Yes - probably much more than the child who is sheltered. Let's look at the value of failure.

10.

How a Child's "Failure" is Feedback

It's a warm day when we visit a large park in the city. Older kids and parents are having great fun; they pump the water cannons and shoot a stream of water at the opponents, manning another pump. Their arms thrust up and down, up and down, trying to build the pressure to send a stream of water rocketing through the air, at their squealing, laughing playmates.

There are shallow paddling pools, tunnels and hills to explore, sand pits and swings and slides. Sophia's brother, Uncle Dan, is the star of the day. Liam has him by the hand, taking him to the swings, then to the seesaw. Liam climbs the ladder of a slide - and whizzes down. The play equipment is bigger and more challenging than in a typical Irish or British playground - children can explore and test their capabilities.

Liam takes his papa by the hand. Alwyn unwinds his lanky body from his relaxed slump on the lawn.

"Over there," points Liam. He leads his papa to the huge stepping-stones which cross the giant pond, to a central island. The distance between the stones is too great for a toddler step. His papa holds his hand and together they navigate the stones. When you are two years old, there is huge learning in jumping from stone to stone. His papa holds his hand and steadies him when he loses balance; he encourages the big jump to the next stone and grabs him upward when he nearly falls.

"I never understood the expression, 'Learning through failure' until I watched my own toddler," muses Sophia. "Look how he's gaining competence, even within a few attempts."

We watch Liam leap from one stepping-stone to the next. He has to be close enough to the edge of the one stone; then launch strongly to gain a footing on the next. Papa supports him when he misjudges. There's a light-hearted play in the interactions between Liam and his papa, as they jump, and slip and recover. There is laughter - not lecture.

Each "failure" is feedback. Liam getting better at doing it each time he tries. Papa follows his lead, letting him absorb the experience, without getting in the way of the learning. *Fun!*

Today is a relaxed time together, but what does a parent do when they need cooperation but the toddler is stubborn?

11.

How to Lead From One Step Behind

There are times when you have an agenda. Perhaps you have an appointment, or you know if you don't get home soon for your child's snack and a nap you will be facing meltdown. You are the parent. You have to make decisions. But you also want to follow your child's lead: what to do?

Shall I distract the child? But then I'm not following their lead.

Let's look at a snapshot of an interaction with a toddler at a time when your agendas may differ - such as when he wants to keep walking in the park and you need to go home.

"Come, Liam, let's go home now."

Liam keeps walking away from us.

"I'm going this way, Liam. Will you push the pushchair?"

Liam keeps walking away from us.

"We can go home and play with the dog in the garden." Liam keeps walking in the opposite direction.

Sometimes when you make the alternative sound more attractive, you can persuade your child to cooperate with your agenda.

And sometimes not.

He may be emotionally attached to his agenda; focused on what has his attention.

Liam keeps walking in the same direction. His gaze is set on a large rock. On this occasion, we don't have a pressing agenda. I follow him.

He tries to clamber onto the rock. Its sides are slippery. He tries again but can't get a grip.

"You want help to climb the rock?"

"Help."

I give him a gentle hoist from behind, so he can clamber up the rock. He stands tall, arms relaxed by his sides, head high.

"You wanted to climb on the rock. You're standing on top!" Liam grins as I "see him". He absorbs his "on the rock" view of the world.

Sophia watches from a distance. When she senses he's satisfied, she calls, "Ok, we can go home now."

Liam slides down the rock and runs towards Mama. We've kept in tune with his agenda. Now he is willing to listen to ours. In the big scheme of things, what matters here? Follow his lead and you'll discover what's important to him. Often it is less stressful and less time-consuming in the long run to gently lead from one step behind, than insist on your agenda. In Ireland there is a saying, "The shortest way round is the longest way home." The more you insist the more they resist. And resistance leads to meltdowns and upsets that can take much longer, and much more energy, to navigate.

Sometimes you have a scheduled commitment that has to take priority. You can still acknowledge your child's reality whilst sticking to your agenda.

"I know you don't want to wear the seatbelt but we all wear seat belts when we go in the car." It might cause meltdown but your agenda has to hold. That is okay. Your relationship is like a bank account. If you have made plenty of deposits along the way, the occasional withdrawal isn't going to cause bankruptcy.

Noticing what matters to your child can make it easier to find a cooperative way forward. Lead from one step behind.

"Do you want to hold teddy or do you want teddy on the seat next to you?" By noticing the small cues of what matters to your child, you can give them enough of a sense of control in the situation for you to usually side-step a power struggle.

You can follow their lead and create a solution that accommodates both your needs. Use your creativity to navigate an interaction - create a solution that keeps you both happy, without disrespecting them as unique persons with their own ideas, desires and needs.

There are times you follow their lead and accommodate what matters to them. This isn't "giving in" when it's your conscious choice. You develop your child's awareness that their experience matters - strengthening their sense of self-agency - they can make a difference in the outcome of the situation. You can give them a sense of control in the situation by giving a simple choice that still achieves your needs, and you can prepare them for the closure of an activity: "We'll walk to the blue bench and then it's time to go home."

Sometimes we can gently re-direct, as Alwyn and I did during an outing - you can read about this in the chapter "When a Toddler Is Fixed On Their Own Agenda".

What to do when you need to keep to your agenda

At times you might need to clearly and firmly stick to your agenda. Don't hook into a power struggle.

Don't over-explain, by repeatedly answering your child's "Why?" If you have already given your answer and your child asks again, unless you have reason to think your child hasn't understood, quietly and firmly repeat your answer, in the same words as before. If he asks again, smoothly answer, "I've already told you that."

You can set a limit without shaming or blaming. If you feel your voice rising or you feel yourself becoming heated, regain your emotional equilibrium.

Use this ABC formula:

Acknowledge to yourself what you are experiencing

Breathe deeply and evenly

Choose to stay calm. For more on this see my book, "Stop Yelling - Nine Steps to Calmer, Happier Parenting".

Sometimes you can redirect the child's attention and at other times they may not like your choice. It happens. And, while they may protest, they also experience you, the parent, are at the helm. Your child needs the safety that you are in control of the situation. When you have intuitively discerned the course you need to take, stick to it. Be the calm your child needs. The relationship you establish with your child now is the foundation for your relationship in later years. Your child needs to know you mean what you say; to know you can be trusted.

As a parent you need to be in control of the situation - which is a different perspective than trying to control the toddler's behaviour! Let's reflect on Mindful Parenting because, when you are mindful, your calmness will give your child a sense of security; and the child who feels secure is more likely to co-operate.

12.

Mindful Parenting - Even When Single-Handed

Sophia and I are both aware I will be leaving in a few weeks and she will be "flying solo" for most of each day. *How is she going to handle a baby and a toddler single-handed?* A mammoth task - enormous, sometimes scary, and hard to handle!

A mammoth task! Since prehistoric times mothers have been in a community, a tribe - not parenting alone. It is a huge task that deserves a support team. It's not only the physical tasks that can be a challenge, but also how to be emotionally present to a toddler whilst also caring for a baby.

- How to give a toddler the physical exercise, the mental stimulation and emotional stability they need?
- How to stay connected when both the toddler and the baby are demanding?
- How to create the routine as well as the flexibility to accommodate everyone's needs?
- How to keep a toddler safe?
- Safe without bubble-wrapping them?
- How to meet the baby's needs too?
- How to still be a person yourself?

There are so many questions that aren't easy to answer. Trust yourself and establish your support base because the task of parenting is too big to do alone. Here are key mindful questions to guide your decision-making in challenging moments.

- "What's needed here?"
- "Do I need to back off and let my child figure this out?"
- "Am I being supportive or am I unhelpfully interfering?"
- "What really matters?"
- "How to create a win-win solution?"

Use these questions to reflect on challenging incidents with your child. You'll find these same questions helpful when they are teenagers, or young adults. Effective parenting is a constant, wise balancing act.

I wish Alwyn could take a few half-days' leave, to create a more gradual ease into the adjustments at home, but that is not possible. When I return home, every weekday Sophia is going to handle this challenge of minding a baby and toddler alone, like millions of other parents around the globe.

I am glad Sophia has already established a group of other mums who will respond when she needs support when Alwyn cannot be there; someone to talk to. Someone who has been through it who can say,

"It will get easier as the weeks go by."

Someone who is going to arrive with a yummy snack, sit and have a cup of coffee and listen to her. Someone who Liam knows and trusts, where he could go play for a few hours, when the need arises.

Someone who will respond when Sophia puts on her Facebook private post to her mothers' group that it has been a tough day today, or a brilliant day.

Sophia trusts herself that she is capable - and trusts herself that her competence as a mother of two will grow day by day. She will figure it out. She will follow her children's lead. They will guide her as to what they need to thrive.

Perhaps you haven't yet developed the confidence you'd like to handle challenging moments with your toddler, or perhaps you still need to create a network of support. in the next chapter you will find key parenting tips on how to follow the child's lead, especially in challenging moments.

13.

Tips On How To Follow Your Child's Lead When It Isn't Easy

Here are suggestions on how to follow your child's lead when it's difficult - at times when you might be tempted to label your child as "naughty" or "bold".

1. Remember the ABC and focus on your breathing

Unless it's an emergency situation where you need to react to keep someone safe, take a moment to:

Acknowledge what's going on for you.

Breathe and choose **C**alm.

Acknowledge - **B**reathe - **C**alm

When you feel your own anger or anxiety rising, focus on slowing and steadying your breathing. When you steady your breathing, it creates a moment to pause. It gives you the chance to stand back from your own strong emotions, and to steady your thoughts. Then you can notice what's needed.

2. Respond rather than react

Think of **react** as in a knee-jerk reaction - instant and without thinking. In any situation you have a split second to determine whether this is an emergency - where you need to **react** to ensure safety - or whether to pause and assess what is most helpful. In most situations, except for emergency concerns, rather than react, it is more helpful to **respond** in a way that gives your child the message, "I'm following you," "I'm here for you." For example, if you react by saying "Don't be bold" or "Don't do that" your child does not understand what they need to do differently, so they are likely to continue with the same behaviour. When you respond, rather than react, you take a moment to first think about how this is for the child. Then you can follow the child's lead and gain insight into what their behaviour is telling you.

3. Your child's behaviour is about them, your response is about you

When your child acts out, they are trying to let you know something is "not ok". It doesn't mean you are a "bad parent". At times when children act out in public, like in the shopping centre, it's easy to feel mortified by their behaviour and then we can easily react, rather than calmly figure out how best to handle the situation.

If you let your thoughts run away with, "What will other people think?" you won't be able to follow your child's lead and you won't recognise what your child's behaviour is trying to tell you. Remember the other's behaviour is about them and their needs. Your response is about you. You will find more about how to respond to your child in the next section.

4. Only say "No" when you absolutely have to

Believe your child is capable. Give opportunities - and unobtrusive help if needed - to develop their competence. For example, often we stop play if it looks a little unsafe but when we do this we may be giving a message,

"You aren't able to do that. You are not big enough. Strong enough. You are not able to figure this out. You are not competent."

Reflect on the situation when Liam climbed the steps on the tractor. Imagine how you might have reacted or responded. What message might you be giving your child? Look for how you can say "Yes!" - by your actions as well as your words. Instead of saying "No, stop that," assess whether this is ok. Or find ways to redirect. Find out more about the power of "yes" in the next chapter - "YOUR EXPERIMENT - Have a 'Yes' Day".

5. Recognise a challenging incident is also an opportunity

An incident can be a learning opportunity for your child and it may also be a opportunity for insight for yourself as parent. It can be a chance to better understand your child; to discover what matters to them, what creates connection and builds your child's self-esteem - what does help, what doesn't and what's needed. It's an opportunity to notice what's unfolding for you as you seek to follow your child's lead.

Click to the "Baby and Toddler Resources" private webpage for readers, where you can download these tips:

https://www.koemba.com/baby-and-toddler-resources/

Print the page and place somewhere to remind you of key points to follow your child's lead, when you most need it.

Now, let's experiment with a "Yes" day!

14.

YOUR EXPERIMENT - Have a "Yes" Day!

Have a yes day!

Try to say "yes" - rather than "no" - to your toddler all day.

If there's a situation where you need to hold a boundary, word it as a "yes" — "Yes, I hear you'd love to …"; "Yes, I see you want to …"

For example your child wants a biscuit before supper.

Instead of saying, "No, we don't eat biscuits before supper,' rather nod and warmly say,

"Yes, You'd like a biscuit. We're going to have a biscuit right after supper."

Acknowledge your child's intention or experience. Name the choice. By offering a choice, you are likely to shift the dynamics and avert a power struggle.

And, just for this experiment, perhaps you might choose to say "yes" to the biscuit before supper!

There are of course situations where you need to hold a boundary, such as if there is a safety concern.

You can still word this as a "yes" -

"Yes, you'd like to go in the road by yourself. And I'm holding your hand."

Unless it is dangerous - unless somebody could get hurt - as far as possible, say "yes" to your toddler's requests for the day.

Forget all the messages of what you "should" do if you're a "good parent". Forget all the things your child is "supposed" to do. Experiment with going with their agenda as far as is reasonable for a day, and see what unfolds. You may be surprised.

- You may be surprised the world doesn't end if you don't say no.
- You may be surprised to realise how many - often unnecessary - times you say no to your toddler.
- You may be surprised how much more relaxed you feel.
- You may be surprised how it dissolves the power struggle and rebalances the family dynamics.
- You may be surprised how much more amenable your toddler becomes.
- You may be surprised how many times you take the lead when you don't need to.

I'm not saying to do this every day. I'm suggesting an experiment - just for one day. Try it!

I didn't try this myself, but Sophia did. She tells me it was magic!

P.S. If you use social media I'd love you to write a post or tweet your experience. Add the hashtags #YesDay and #BabyAndToddlerOnBoard and other readers of this book will be able to enjoy it too!

In the next chapter we'll reflect on how to follow the baby's lead.

15.

Follow Your Baby's Lead

I gaze at my gorgeous new granddaughter snuggled in my arms. She gives a yawn - I open and close my mouth in the same shape "yawn". She gazes at me and I return her gaze. Her precious little fingers curl around my one finger, which seems gigantic compared to hers - I keep my finger gently still so it's easy for her to hold. Without realising it, I'm following her lead.

In this book the focus is on the toddler. But of course, there is also another important little person in the family - your baby. So we'll take a chapter in each section to look at how these three key insights can help create an environment for your baby to thrive:

- Follow your child's lead

- Cross the bridge

- "Hearth" your home

Recognise your baby is already a sensate being

Our understanding of what babies need to thrive has developed significantly since I trained as a teacher in the 1970s. The general viewpoint in education and in parenting then was babies come into this world as "empty vessels" that needed to be filled with knowledge. Now we are so much more aware babies are sensate beings even before they are born. The reasoning part of the young child's brain is not yet developed but they already are connecting with us. This means from the very beginning they sense our mood, whether we are stressed, upset, happy or relaxed. Babies are aware how we interact with them and how we interact with others. (I've watched a baby cry and cry, refusing any comfort until his mother and father stopped arguing and calmed down.)

Some babies' experience of life is of people who are loving - connecting with them and meeting their needs. Sadly some babies experience alone-ness, no-one responding consistently to their emotional needs. A baby can't verbalise these experiences - which are encoded as implicit memories, and these may stay with them throughout their life, without any conscious awareness.

Even though language is not yet developed, the little person's experiences of met or unmet needs begin to form their perception of life. They don't yet have the words to articulate what they are experiencing but they are forming an impression of whether or not their world is a safe, predictable and loving place. How we interact with babies is laying a foundation that all later interactions and learning will be built upon.

Tune in to your baby's cues

When we follow the child's lead we become more attuned to their experience and their ways of communicating. The cues your baby gives you are signals to guide you to what your baby needs, helping you to respond. Your baby gazes at you, holds the gaze or looks away, their eyes follow something else, their body tightens or relaxes, they reach out, use different cries, little sighs, snuffles and grunts, indicating their different needs. Take time to notice how much your baby is sharing about how they experiencing their world. And as you respond to your baby's cues they develop a preverbal awareness of the communication between you.

Build connection with your baby

You can consciously build rapport with your baby, as you can with your toddler. Baby gazes at you - you gaze back. Baby makes a particular expression - you mirror it. Right from the word go, give your baby a sense, "I see you", "I'm here with you."

When you follow and respond to your baby's lead, you will discover how and what they are communicating. Of course, when you start noticing the nonverbal signals of your baby you will also become more aware of the non-verbal signals of your other loved ones. And at the same time, by honing your skills to follow your toddler's lead you will find you also become more attuned to follow your baby's lead.

As you're already well aware, your baby will need a great deal of your attention. That time is a gift to develop a strong bond between the two of you, as you attend to your baby's needs, follow your baby's gaze, and mirror facial expressions and gestures. Your toddler is more independent, but may be struggling with the huge adjustment, and needs this close attention as well. It is a challenge to stay attuned to both, especially when you might be in need of a good sleep yourself. Yet engaging meaningfully with your toddler and your baby, as best as you are able, can maintain the connection and emotional equilibrium your children need - and that leads to happier interactions for everyone in the family.

If other adults in your support group are aware of the importance of this attunement, they can help by giving quality time to one of the children, or dealing with some of the practical things in the home, so you have one-on-one time with your other child, or a much-needed rest.

So, holding both your baby and your toddler in mind, let's take a quick review of how to follow your child's lead.

16.

Follow Your Child's Lead - Recap

We've looked at different ways in which you can follow your child's lead:

- in being present to your child's experience

- in simple interactions

- in art activities

- in play

- in what matters to the child

- in risking "failure".

Following the child's lead matters because the child is a unique individual, whose development is so rapid, their needs and abilities change day by day.

"Oops - Are you there now!" — we can often be surprised by our child's spurts of development and growing interests and abilities.

A situation where everything flowed yesterday may be a different story today. As one mum said, "Each time I think I have this parenting thing sorted, my toddler pulls the rug from under my feet, and I'm starting all over again."

This isn't bad news, though it may be bewildering and up-setting. It is good news because it means they are making healthy developmental progress.

Following my grandson's lead tuned me in to his pace. Instead of rushing forward with my agenda, and then wondering why the toddler protests, following the child's lead has slowed me down, to take his experience into account. It slowed me down to come alongside him. Our connectedness grew. We were flowing together because I followed his lead.

In this next section we'll "cross the bridge" into the world of toddler-dom- imagining life through the eyes of your child. We'll discover why this especially matters for your toddler as they adjust to home with a baby on board.

SECTION B

CROSS THE BRIDGE

If we are to reach real peace in the world,
we shall have to begin with the children.

Gandhi

17.

Cross the Bridge - Introduction

In our second step, we'll explore how to cross the bridge in everyday situations — to see life from the toddler's viewpoint and respond from this perspective. What do I mean by crossing the bridge? I mean choosing to mentally reposition yourself in the world of toddler-dom, so you can gain a sense of how life is from your child's point of view. That's easier said than done. It means I have to "park" my own agenda, my own busy-ness and own anxiety; my own paradigm, prejudices and judgements about whether this behaviour is "ok". I can't connect with his experience if I'm focused on life on my side of the bridge.

We'll look at:

- How to cross the bridge when challenging behaviours arise
- Why punishment doesn't work, why discipline does - and how they are different
- Giving choices
- Being present to the toddler's emotional experience
- How to support the child when other adults don't cross the bridge
- When a toddler won't listen

Let's look at how we cross the bridge, so we can view the situation, not through our adult eyes but through the eyes of the toddler. This is important because we can respond to the child's needs when we perceive their perspective. Then we'll discover how to create the win-win solutions that both toddler and parent need to thrive.

18

Why Crossing The Bridge Matters

Liam loves going into the greenhouse to pick the tiny, rich red tomatoes. He hands some to me and we both enjoy the soft, juicy texture and taste of the sun-warmed fruit. We put more in our mouths than in the basket. The plants thrive in the warm humid conditions of the greenhouse. I think about the similarity between gardening and parenting.

A gardener knows he needs to create the ideal conditions for a plant to thrive. If a plant looks miserable, he doesn't grumble at the plant. He doesn't tell it to "behave". He figures out what adjustments to make - more shade, more nutrients, drier soil - it's different for each plant. He thinks about what is needed from the plant's perspective. If a plant is straggly, miserable and stunted, or masses of leaves but no flowers - the gardener knows these are signs the plant needs something different. Plants won't thrive if we ignore what they need. In the same way as the mindful gardener observes and learns what is needed for each plant to flourish, through our interactions we gain insight to our child's perspective. We cross the bridge to figure out what each child uniquely needs, to grow to their full potential.

It's helpful to get into the habit of crossing the bridge during positive or neutral interactions, rather than waiting till challenging issues arise to develop this skill.

Perhaps your toddler says,

"I love Thomas the Tank Engine."

Unthinkingly, we might comment,

"Yes, come drink your juice now." Or, "Yes - and you love the other trains too." Those comments are made with good intent, but we aren't in tune with what the child is focusing on right now. Cross the bridge into their world. They aren't thinking about juice. They aren't necessarily thinking about the other trains.

Experiment with crossing the bridge. Get down to the child's eye level, alongside them. Let your eyes follow where their gaze is resting. Notice the child's focus. See what they see. Try to imagine what they are experiencing. Mirror their words - "You love Thomas Tank Engine." Let your voice, energy, your pace and your body language be in rapport with your child. Stay present to your child. They will sense when you are connecting with their world.

It's a challenge to move from the parenting mode we've known all our lives to seeing life from the child's perspective. A great way to practise this skill is using playdough. Sit alongside or opposite your child. Give yourself an equal size ball of fresh playdough to the amount your child has. Whatever they do with the playdough, do the same with your playdough. Mirror what they say, or do what they ask you to do. As far as possible, follow their lead. Resist the urge to use your playdough to show them how to do it "better". Don't initiate any new ideas or conversation; just observe what your child is doing and expressing, and mirror. Notice your experience as you do this and notice what happens in the space between you.

When you cross the bridge into your child's world by mirroring or verbalising their experience you develop your awareness of your toddler's vantage point. It also develops the child's budding sense of self - of being seen and having a sense of "feeling felt" within *their* experience of life.

Practise crossing the bridge, to notice your child's positive, everyday experiences. Then, at times when relationships are strained and your toddler acts out, you'll have the communication skills to connect when it's not easy, and when it matters the most. Like the gardener, we need the know-how and the skills to create the environment for healthy growth. And part of that essential knowledge is a clear understanding of the difference between punishment and discipline, if we want our children to thrive. Let's observe an eating-out situation.

19

Why Punishment Doesn't Work - Why Discipline Does

We're treating ourselves to coffee in the nearby town.

'Do you want to sit in the high chair or do you want to sit on the chair next to me?' Sophia asks Liam.

Liam chooses to sit on the chair next to her and drives his toy car along the surface of the table, while we wait for the waitress to bring our drinks.

A man comes in with his two boys, the younger about the same age as Liam and the other a few years older. The bigger lad sits in a chair at the table alongside us. Without saying anything to the toddler, the dad swings him off his feet, to put him into the high chair. The child lets out a roar of protest and stiffens his body like a plank. The dad struggles to manoeuvre the wailing child's rigid body into the high chair. Once the child is in the high chair, he gives the child his phone to look at. The child throws the phone to the floor and cries louder. An elderly lady shakes her head and rolls her eyes towards the ceiling

In desperation the dad lifts the toddler out of the highchair and places him in the chair by the window. The child relaxes. His crying stops, he eases back in the chair, gazing at the traffic outside and munching on his food.

At first, this dad didn't follow his child's lead. When a toddler protests it's easy to react. "Stop this behaviour!"

"Be a good boy," we grumble or cajole.

"Sit and eat your food and then we'll go to the park," we coerce.

"Now sit in the chair or we're going straight home," we threaten.

When we stay on the adult side of the bridge and ignore the child's experience, our reaction is to try to get our child to "behave!"

But this dad recognised his child's protest. He crossed the bridge into the child's world. The child wanted to sit by the window in a big chair, like everyone else. The child wasn't misbehaving - he was letting his dad know he needed something different. That dad could have made his own life easier if he had paused sooner to consider his child's perspective. He could have said to his child,

"Can I lift you into the high chair?" Sometimes we don't ask our children questions like this because we think they don't have the vocabulary, but they understand much more than they can articulate. Even if the dad overlooked the opportunity to create cooperation, it would have been easier for them both if he had responded to the first signs of protest. As he lifted him and the child stiffened his body, the father could have responded to the child's protest. He had the opportunity to pause and make eye contact with his son. He might have said,

"Uh, oh. You don't want to sit in the high chair?"

The father could have given him a choice.

"Would you like to sit in the high chair, or in the chair next to me?"

His son would sense his father crossing the bridge. Together they could figure out what was needed. This makes life easier, and many small incidents of connection and cooperation make a huge difference in the child's experience of life. A child who has to battle for their corner may grow up believing the world is a tough and unsafe place. But when a child "feels felt" - when they sense you are entering into their experience - they experience life as secure. The message your interactions give are,

"Your experience matters. *You* matter!"

When you cross the bridge and see the situation from the child's perspective, you will often be able to figure out a way for you and your child to cooperate, before the situation reaches meltdown. It's an essential part of being a toddler to test the boundaries. That's how they make sense of the world.

When a child's behaviour needs guiding

You might have to stop a particular behaviour - hurting the baby, doing something that could be dangerous - it's *how* you discipline that counts. Some parents resort to time-out, whether you term that the "naughty chair", the "bold step" or whatever. They think it works because the child complies. But what about the child's experience? Cross the bridge. Imagine how your child feels when there's been an upset and you isolate them. Imagine how you would feel if your friends or colleagues ignored you. Imagine how much worse this would be if you are reliant upon the person who excludes you. You might stop the behaviour but how does the child feel? Probably they feel confused, frustrated, deeply sad and cut off from you. This isn't a helpful foundation to build a relationship of connection and cooperation. It might "work" for the parent but I don't believe it ever "works" for the child.

Why time-out is not okay

Time-out is not discipline. Time-out is punishment. Punishment tries to control and evokes fear. Cross the bridge and imagine how time-out feels for your child, especially when they are placed "out" while the baby is "in" with the parent! What might that experience be for the older sibling? The isolation of time-out can feel like abandonment. Think about a young wild mammal. If the mother does not return it will probably die. The infant creature cannot survive without care. When a parent uses tactics the child experiences as abandonment, this is such an overwhelming state for the young child, it can feel as though "I'm going to die." When a child experiences panic their behaviour will be reactive. They'll be in a state of anxiety; they'll try to create reconnection, at whatever cost; they may misbehave to gain your attention. Or they might give up their own needs in desperation to reconnect; they may resort to compliance and say sorry when they don't mean it. They may go along with your agenda, but what meta message, will stay with them? We store implicit memories even though we do not consciously remember them. How might a repeated feeling of abandonment impact their inner sense of security and well-being - both now and in adulthood. Let's be aware that if we leave the child alone on the other side of the bridge they may be hearing, "You deserve isolation."

Let's take a quick look at neuroscience to see why time-out isn't a helpful parenting approach. The deep part of the brain, known as the "reptilian brain"or amygdala, is programmed for survival. Our brains are still running on the same programme as our primitive ancestors' did. When something feels threatening the reptilian brain is triggered. This activated reptilian brain overrides the cortex - the part of the brain which logically processes our experiences. This means our reasoning ability is temporarily offline. If the child experiences a sense of abandonment, they'll be stressed, and their brain won't be able to process the situation. They might learn how to avoid this pain again, but they won't develop the social skills that can be gained when we model kinder and more helpful ways of responding. They won't take any significant learning from this situation to develop their reasoning capacity to deal with other similar scenarios.

Why discipline is different to punishment

I'm sure you want to support your child's developing competence as a reasoning, responsible, and caring person. As parents, rather than reacting in a way that sparks our child's "fight, fight or freeze" survival mechanisms, we need to cultivate cooperative interactions that are mutually respectful, rather than impose a punitive approach.

Discipline and punishment are not the same thing. Punishment attempts to exert control over the child, and evokes fear, which will trigger your child's reactive, reptilian brain. Discipline is different - it works from the inside out. Discipline means you're responding from a whole-brain approach, responding to what's needed, rather than reacting in a coercive or punitive way. Discipline nurtures the child's capability to develop healthy self-discipline. When you discipline from a calm, centred place, your child is far less likely to become reactive. And even if they do have a toddler meltdown, you can choose not to hook into the reactive behaviour. At times when a child's behaviour is most demanding is when they most need your calm connection. When your child seems most unlovable is when they most need your love.

Why a parent needs to set limits

A mindful parent holds boundaries in a way that respects everyone's well-being, including the toddler's. Healthy discipline encourages family cooperation by holding the boundaries needed to keep all concerned physically and emotionally safe. Your child needs you to set clear, consistent limits, to maintain their sense of security - "Mama/Papa has things in hand."

Sometimes a parent mistakes indulgence for love. The child demands and the parent gives, and gives, and gives - without setting limits - until eventually the parent's patience runs thin. In seconds this kind, tolerant parent morphs into mean monster-parent:

"I said 'NO!' - Why don't you listen!

What's wrong with you!

Stop that silly behaviour - Now!"

If you become reactive, if you lose the cool, who is there to keep your child safe? Imagine how it might feel for a child if one moment you're in "Yes dear, whatever you want, dear" mode but the next you're yelling or punishing. What does that do for your child's sense of self? What does it do for your relationship? What does it do for their developing awareness of how people interact?

I wasn't always the parent I wanted to be. I didn't often lose the cool with my kids, but I can remember feeling so bad when I did. I'd grumble at myself, "I mustn't get angry again." It was years later I learnt about Emotional Intelligence and discovered anger is a signal I need change. Rather than try not to feel angry, I learnt to listen to what my anger was telling me. And often I recognised I wasn't taking the time or space to mind myself well enough. Once I listened and responded to what my anger was telling me I found the emotion naturally dissipated. A parent "loses the cool" when too much of herself - or himself - has been compromised for too long. Recognise your feeling of anger is calling you to set limits for your well-being, as well as for your child's.

Another challenge with not setting clear boundaries is we might overcompensate when we have calmed down, because we are feeling guilty about the way we handled the situation. We're in danger of creating an emotional rollercoaster, rather than a "home with hearth". We'll talk more about this in the next section.

A child with no boundaries won't have safety and will experience anxiety. The fine line a parent needs to hold when crossing the bridge is to recognise what the child needs, what they are trying to explore and express - yet remain the loving, calm, assertive parent. This is not something to quantify in "ten tips to discipline a toddler" - as much as our left-brain logic would like. It's about being whole-brained parents; engaging our logic and reasoning as well as our compassion and intuition. We need to be calm to assess what's needed in each situation.

Why boundaries matter

Mindful Parenting of a toddler isn't easy. It's not about letting the toddler do whatever they please. A child without boundaries feels emotionally unsafe — they need your guidance. If we resort to coercion or punishment, we take the adult's viewpoint into account but ignore the child's perspective.

Will your approach to limit-setting impact your child to believe no-one cares what they think - no-one understands. Will they believe if they don't follow other people's agenda they may be cut off? Or will the way you hold boundaries help your child learn *every* person matters?

Mindful Parenting is about crossing the bridge, developing connection and communication, and using healthy discipline to set limits to create an environment where the family thrives.

So what does a parent do when a toddler won't cooperate?

20.

Give Your Toddler Choices

"Do you want to walk to the shop or do you want to sit in the pushchair?"

"Do you want apple or banana?"

I love the way Sophia and Alwyn give Liam choices.

Choices are a respectful way of negotiating with a toddler. Choices work because we cross the bridge - we take his needs into account too. His needs are acknowledged. We find a way to create cooperation.

We're about to go on an outing and I ask Liam, "Shall I come in the car too?"

Sophia exclaims,

"Are you going to stay behind if he says no!"

I grin. I'm confident he wants me to come - but of course a choice is a choice!

Give choices to your toddler

Too many choices for a toddler can be overwhelming. As parents, we need to figure out what are the big issues we need to decide and what are the everyday choices the child can make independently.

It's easier for the child to decide between only two things. So, for example, instead of saying,

"What do you want to eat?" it's more helpful to say,

"Do you want yoghurt or a sandwich?"

One choice. An easier decision for a toddler.

"Red shirt or blue?"

"Which book do you want to read?" while you have two favourite books in your hands they're likely to choose — of course, they might run to fetch a different book; that's okay.

When you need to, hold a boundary

Giving a choice isn't always an option. In an emergency situation, where the child or somebody else could be in danger, you react to ensure safety. Today Liam tests the limit and runs out of the garden onto the pavement. I'm quick to catch him; I clasp his hand, and guide him inside the gate.

"The pavement is not the place for playing. We play in the garden."

My voice and my actions are calm and firm, setting the limit.

The toddler needs you, the parent, in charge when it comes to safety issues.

How and when to use choices with your toddler

As a mindful parent, you're aware not all choices are equal.

"Do you want to go to the shops?"

That's okay if your child can choose to stay home or go with you. But if you let them decide the family agenda, you put too much pressure on them. The child needs *you* to be the Alpha leader - calm and in control of the situation. Not authoritarian - but calm-assertive. The *parent* needs to make the key decisions. Your child won't always like that. They might protest at times. But your child will feel more secure when they know you are making the significant decisions. You can still reflect their experience-how they experience life from their side of the bridge, and give a choice you can accommodate:

"You want to play. We need to go to the shop. Would you like to bring one of your toys with you?"

When you acknowledge your child's desire and give a choice, it can hold the equilibrium in a challenging moment. This is important because you are seeing the world from their perspective and responding to what they need.

When your toddler has a meltdown

You toddler might have a meltdown - toddlers sometimes do - but you don't have to react; you can choose to stay calm. A child's behaviour is about them; your response is about you. They need you to stay calm because the toddler's brain is still too immature for them to calm themselves. They need you to contain their big emotions. Not to shut them down, but to gently contain them when they feel overwhelmed. Your child might rage and roar for a while but, when they sense your calm, connected presence, the huge wave of emotion will subside. Be the calm your child needs.

We'll return to the topic of tantrums in the next section. For now, let's hold in mind the young child needs you to create emotional safety and to narrate their experience. Let's look at other ways we can cross the bridge to create the connection your toddler needs.

21.

When Your Toddler Feels Jealous

Sophia had shared with me that she recognises that Liam does not have to be happy about the baby's arrival. If we suggest emotions he's not feeling, we'll confuse him. If a child says, "I don't like the baby," and we say,

"Of course you do, you love your sister," we negate the reality he's experiencing. We need to cross the bridge and see moment by moment how he is experiencing the situation. He needs support with whatever emotions he is feeling. Emotions aren't right or wrong; they are the compass to navigate relationship. We can respond to his experience.

"You don't like the baby. Tell me more." When we cross the bridge we listen to the child's experience. Rather than try to persuade the child to like the new sibling, acknowledge their emotions and respond to their needs. This is all unfamiliar territory for the child and they are trying to comprehend this big change in their world. Even if there are other people to give attention, life is not as it was, and at times this will trigger the reptilian brain - it makes sense the toddler will have emotional reactions.

The child's behaviour can give us important feedback about how they are with the changes in the home. Tonight Sophia is holding baby Anna; Liam wants to cuddle too. Sophia opens her arm to include him. Liam stops. He pulls back. He needs his Mama to himself. Sophia asks me if baby Anna can have a "Granny cuddle". My being there makes it easier for Sophia to give Liam undivided attention; she gives him "yours-and-yours-alone" cuddle time. She crosses the bridge. Give him what he needs.

Are we "giving in" to the toddler?

Many parents take the attitude that they should not "give in" and they think the toddler needs to "get used to this". But how is this experience when you look at it through the toddler's eyes? Their life experience has been, "Mama is mine." Now they see parents giving smiles, coos and cuddles to another child. The toddler needs time and support to accept there's another member in the family, and to develop a happy relationship with this little person.

It makes sense they feel anxious or unhappy sometimes. There may be moments when they feel angry about sharing their parents. They need reassurance; reassurance their needs are met too. They matter too. And most of all, they need reassurance from the ones who have been the centre of their universe - their parents.

Sophia and Alwyn have discussed how they want to handle this transition. They want to cross the bridge; to respond empathetically to his experience, whether he's feeling loving towards the baby, happy, sad, confused or angry. Papa can have huge impact at this time. Papa can become the toddler's number one ally.

Parenting isn't meant to be a solo endeavour, or a couple's job. Parenting for thousands of years has been a family affair, a community project. It's such an important job - having the support of a team who are committed to your child's well-being is hugely beneficial. I'm glad I'm here. Right now a key part of this child-raising endeavour is to support a toddler through the transition of a sibling's arrival.

Cross the bridge so you can be present to the toddler and see how they see the situation. Cross the bridge so they can weave their experience into the rich fabric of their life. In the next chapter we'll chat about an expression used in many homes that can have huge implications for your toddler, which you may never have thought about.

22

Don't Have a "New" Baby

Don't have a "new baby" - just have a "baby".

I was taught this by a four year old. This child turned to her mother and asked,

"Mummy, when you get the new baby, what happens to me?"

Oh wow. Think of it. When you get the new car, the new sofa, the new TV - what happens to the old one? It's discarded!

This helped me to see one little word - "new"' - can create feelings of insecurity or jealousy for a child at the arrival of a sibling.

When we cross the bridge into the child's world, we see how they may feel anxious or threatened when a baby becomes part of the family. Life is no longer what it was, no matter how beautiful the baby. Some toddlers tell the parents to send the baby back. *I want you to myself!*

Hopefully it's going to be an even happier family - but your child doesn't know that yet. Love and bonding are not a given and can take time for siblings.

I think about other situations I've observed. When a child is unhappy about the baby, a parent sometimes reacts with a comment,

"Of course you love your baby brother!"

That's not the child's experience, in this moment, when they express anger or upset. The child might feel loving ten minutes from now, but right now love isn't what they're feeling. Rather, put words on the child's experience: "You're angry?", "You're upset?" Your toddler needs to know you are seeking to understand their experience. They need to *feel felt*.

Sophia and Alwyn show the child's perspective matters too. When Liam needs attention, when Mama is the only one he wants, either Alwyn or I take over the baby-care so they can respond to Liam's need. For any parent of two little ones, it's helpful to have an extra tuned-in person, especially in the early days, so there is a caregiver to respond to each child's needs.

That raises another question, which we'll look at in the next chapter: "How can I support my child when other adults don't cross the bridge?"

23.

When a Toddler Feels Left Out

Baby Anna is gorgeous. With her mop of dark, curly hair and soft, smooth skin she looks like a live doll. I watch how friends and relatives respond when they meet the family. "She's a beautiful baby." they coo over the pram, whilst Liam stands alongside. *What about her brother - he's gorgeous too!*

"Aren't you lucky to have a sister!" *I wish they'd cross the bridge!* Some siblings might be delighted to have a baby arrive, but we can't presume a child is happy about the baby. How can a toddler process his feelings about this big development in his life, if adults impose words such as "happy" and "lucky"? Denied emotions might go under cover but they don't go away. They will implode or explode. Challenging behaviours - shyness, non-co-operation, whining and tantrums - are signs the toddler needs support. And his experience of a baby in the house is impacted by the way others interact.

What can a parent do to minimise the impact of well-meaning people who don't notice the toddler's needs? How to respond to people who aren't aware of crossing the bridge? I find it helps to engage Liam's attention; we go play with the toy trains or feed the ducks. Or respond to comments in a way that affirms your toddler:

"Thank you. We're so happy to have two gorgeous children now!"

Sophia and Alwyn are mindful of Liam as a unique individual on his own journey through life. They are aware of life from his perspective and his emotional reaction. They acknowledge Liam's experience and affirm him as the child they love. But that doesn't mean any behaviour is okay. What can a parent do when a toddler's behaviour is challenging?

24.

What To Do When a Toddler Acts Out

What to do when the toddler acts out? That's a heart-cry from many parents. Just because we strive to see life from their perspective doesn't mean there aren't challenges.

- Hurting the baby,
- tantrums,
- not eating,
- reverting to less mature behaviour,
- becoming frequently ill.

All these can be signs your child is having difficulty adjusting to the baby being part of the family. What can a parent do? Hear and respond to the "SOS" your toddler is sending, rather than trying to "make them behave."

We need to hold a firm limit in the face of acting-out behaviour. If they hurt the baby, they need a firm reminder of "gentle hands", and how we give that message matters. The child needs you to stay the calm assertive parent, holding the limit without becoming reactive.

Maybe your child thinks, "They love the baby more than me."

Imagine how that unloved feeling escalates if we shame and scold the child for "bad" behaviour. If the child's sense of self is demeaned, they're likely to act mean!

If we see the situation through the child's eyes, we'll reflect on what might lie behind the behaviour. What do they need to reassure and support them at this time, to release the inner tension, which leads to misbehaving? They need reassurance they are loved — they matter. When they act out, it is a cry for your attention. And because their young brain is still "under construction" they often can't process or verbally express what they are experiencing.

The toddler brain processes a message:

> *"Mama loves the baby.*
> *My survival in danger.*
> *Cortex bypass invoked.*
> *Full control diverted to amygdala."*

Result - toddler meltdown.

When you say something like, "Don't be naughty" it exacerbates the child's feelings of anger or alone-ness; of no-one being alongside them in their world. When you scold or threaten, the message your child hears is, "You're not okay." The child may feel unseen – "No-one understands." At a time when the toddler may already be feeling left out, they especially need the parent to cross the bridge and come alongside their emotional experience.Your words may get in the way of giving what they need. Perhaps drawing the child towards you for a soft hug will ease their tension - and yours. When the tension is eased, challenging behaviours often naturally disappear.

When your toddler's physical and emotional needs - and yours! - are met, it can go a long way to creating a smooth transition. And it can make for a more harmonious relationship between siblings later. But toddler tantrums can still erupt. We'll look at how to contain big emotions in our third step. In the meantime, let's look at how crossing the bridge into the toddler's world can ease potentially challenging situations.

25.

What To Do When A Toddler Gets Stubborn

Imagine when a parent's attitude is inflexible and the tone is authoritarian — where the child's experience is ignored:

"You can't go outside without your pants. Put on your pants **now**! Are you listening to me! Put them on now! Okay - then you can't go in the garden!" This type of interaction often leads to a toddler's stubborn behaviour, to tears, frustration, upset or meltdown. The more you insist, the more they resist. If a child acts in a stubborn way, they may be trying to tell you,

"You're ignoring what I am trying to express."

Compare a mindful interaction, spoken gently with warmth and patience:

"You want to go in the garden? Then you need to put on your pants. Okay - you're going to put on your pants! Which pants do you want, your blue pants or your brown pants? Okay, you want your brown pants."

Sophia and Alwyn cross the bridge - seeking to see life from Liam's perspective - they make the small adjustments which give him a sense of control within his environment. The tone is warm and relaxed.

When you cross the bridge into your child's experience, and respond so your child senses you are trying to see things as they do, you are more likely to achieve a win/win solution where your needs are met as well as your child's. It's not only the words you use but how you say it. The tone of crossing the bridge is kinder:

"Can you get a plate for your food, please."

Liam opens the cupboard door. His eating utensils are at his height. *Oh! That's why his things are in the drawer where I have to bend to reach them.* Sophia and Alwyn create a child-friendly environment, where he can see and reach what he needs. They strive to see the world from his eyes. They encourage his self-agency - his ability to do things for himself and to make choices. When he can help himself, he develops his competence and he can bring about the change he needs. He isn't at the whim of chance and he's not solely reliant on a parent's help. He learns to manage little day-to-day activities in his own life. Sophia and Alwyn cross the bridge by understanding their toddler wants to learn to do things; they empower him to do things for himself. This encourages his physical and mental development and it also reduces his frustration, which means he's less likely to act out, and there's a calmer ebb and flow in their interactions.

Toddlers need a sense of control about their own selves. This is key to smoother more cooperative relationships.

Toddlers do get frustrated. They do have meltdowns.

They want to do things but they aren't able. Or they are stopped.

They want to communicate something. They can't.

The frustration builds. Meltdown happens.

A child's anger signals they want change. Their frustration makes sense because there are things they want to express they can't make you understand; there are things they want to do but they can't. At times when your child isn't cooperating, they aren't being naughty or stubborn. They are trying to let you know their needs. You'll find it more helpful to shift your focus from trying to control their behaviour; rather cross the bridge and visualise how your child might experience the situation. When we imagine life from their perspective, we can adapt our approach to accommodate their experience as well as ours. There will be challenging parenting moments - they are still toddlers and you are a parent with a busy schedule and other things on your mind. The young child's brain and body are undergoing continuous development that isn't always easy for us to comprehend, so it makes sense turbulence comes with the territory of toddlerhood. When we cross the bridge, we can see and respond to what's needed, and this means we'll have less chaos and more calm in the home. So what to do when toddler won't listen?

26.

When a Toddler Is Fixed On Their Agenda

It's Saturday and Alwyn is home today. He and I decide to take a walk with Liam to the nearby playground. We take the pushchair with us in case Liam tires on the return trip. It's about a kilometre stroll. The roadworks team isn't working today but the diggers are parked in the field alongside the path to the park. Liam grabs Papa's hand and points. Liam gazes at the grey digger, the little white one and the enormous yellow digger, towering over us like frozen prehistoric creatures. When he has absorbed this we remind him of the big green slide in the playground.

When we arrive at the park, I sit on the bench, soaking up the idle autumn sun and let Alwyn take toddler-duty. While Liam loads sand into a tipper truck Alwyn comes and sits beside me. We chat about the garden project we're busy with.

Liam toddles over to us. He eats a piece of apple and takes a few sips of water. He wants his Papa to push him on the swing.

Back and forth. Back and forth. Back and forth.

What is it about a swing that is so soothing!

Alwyn glances at his phone.

"I think we need to get going, We can stop at the shop on our way home."

Most days "Go to the shops" has immediate appeal to Liam. But today this doesn't work. He runs to the sand.

"Come, Liam, we need to go see Mama now."

Liam whimpers. He wants to play with the tipper truck. How are we going to leave the playground without a meltdown? It's nearly lunchtime. An upset will erupt if he gets too hungry.

But he's determined to stay in the playground.

When we came I'd left the pushchair near the playground gate.

"Liam, please put the water bottle in the pushchair."

He takes the bottle to the pushchair. Alwyn realises I'm manoeuvring towards the gate and he grabs our belongings.

"Look at the flower, Liam." The large bright daisy further along the path catches his attention. He runs to sniff it. We're out the gate now.

"Let's go see the diggers!"

We're under way. He's getting tired and he climbs into the pushchair. We chat about the diggers as we pass. Then I remind him of the next anticipation,

"Let's see if the train is coming."

"Red train, red train," he squeals in delight as we near the railway bridge.

Soon we are home to Mama.

We could have had a power struggle on our hands. Today "Let's go to the shop," didn't work. It does other days, but not today. By being present to the situation, we figured a way to change the focus of his attention. We crossed the bridge into his reality and led from one step behind. With a toddler it's never a "one-size-fits-all" approach. Even with the same child, emotions fluctuate and situations change; you need to be present, imaginative and flexible to create flow. What works in one situation might not work in the next. We need to cross the bridge moment by moment to figure out how the toddler is seeing life, if we want to happily navigate toddler-dom.

27

Tips To Cross the Bridge When It Isn't Easy

Crossing the bridge sounds easy but it's often more challenging than we realise. Our own thoughts often get in the way of us crossing the bridge. We see our own agenda as the priority. At times, our agenda is urgent, but our flexibility and our creativity in handling frustrating moments can make a big difference to the outcome.

Our thoughts can be barriers in other ways too:

We have self-judging thoughts.

"I'm not a good parent." "I can't do this."

We worry about what others think.

We sometimes have negative perceptions about our child.

"She's trying to wind me up." "She's being a brat."

These thoughts are unhelpful. They get in your way of seeing possibilities. They block you from crossing the bridge into your child's experience.

This section of the book builds on following child's lead, so you might find it helpful to review the five tips at the end of the previous section. Here are five tips to help you cross the bridge when it isn't easy.

1. Recognise your own emotions

If you're feeling frustrated, overwhelmed, anxious, annoyed or angry, then you are in your own headspace and it's not possible to cross the bridge to your child's world. In challenging times, our emotions often grab the steering wheel of our interaction and can land our relationships in topsy-turvy places, and exasperate the behaviours we would like to curtail.

Focus on your breathing, inwardly acknowledge your own emotional state, and choose to respond - rather than react.

2. Choose your thoughts

When you notice you're having a strong reaction, focus on your breathing and notice what's happening in your mind. The key question:

"Is this thought winding me up or helping me steer the interaction to a win-win solution?"

Reactive thoughts create barriers to crossing the bridge to your child's world. Seek thoughts that calm and connect you.

3. Seek to understand what your child's behaviour could be telling you

When we cross the bridge and see the situation from their perspective, it's easier to understand a toddler's behaviour, and then we can respond in a supportive way. Notice whenever you want to label your child's behaviour. Instead of thinking they're "bad", "defiant" - or whatever other label jumps into your head - focus on what your child's experience might be in this moment. Discover what's needed to restore equilibrium, in a way that supports the child's development and also the family's well-being - which includes *you*! Your child wants to connect and be in your good graces but sometimes they do it in counter-productive ways. Sometimes your child might try to pick up the baby, or "tidy the kitchen'" for you and cause chaos. When you look for the child's positive intent behind the behaviour, it's easier to be patient and to respond helpfully.

4. Verbalise your child's experience

When you verbalise what your child is doing/experiencing, you notice where they are, both physically and their inner world; this is the first step to crossing the bridge. You become more aware of their intention, their experience and their emotions. This helps when you need to redirect a behaviour or set a limit, because you find yourself in a different head-space when you connect with their experience. When you get into the habit of first verbalising their experience, you develop a key skill to building connection because you can't articulate what you have not observed.

It's also helpful for your child, because as they build their vocabulary, they'll have other tools to express themselves. For example, they will learn they can say, "I'm angry" rather than throwing something at you.

For example, you want your child to come to the table and she is playing with her dolls.

"I see you're playing with your dolls. You're having fun. Supper is nearly ready so we'll need to come to the table in a few minutes. Can you tell your dolls you're coming for your supper soon!"

You'll find life goes more smoothly when you connect with the child's experience and prepare the child for the change which is about to come. You may have your agenda, but first see where they are at and weave the two sides together.

5. Recognise "My child is doing the best they can right now"

Stay in the mindset,

"This is the best my child is able to do in this moment." Maybe your child has a tantrum. It doesn't mean you like that behaviour. It doesn't mean you don't wish they would do differently. But when you recognise, "They're doing the best they can right now," you'll move from a focus of judgement and control to rebuilding connection. We'll look at that in the next section.

Click to the "Baby and Toddler Resources" private webpage for readers, where you can download these tips:

https://www.koemba.com/baby-and-toddler-resources/

Print the page and place somewhere to remind you of key points to cross the bridge to your child, when you most need it.

Don't miss the next chapter because I'll share a crossing the bridge experiment that could give you insights you've never seen before!

28.

YOUR EXPERIMENT - Using Visualisation to Reframe Negative Experiences

You will need to plan at least twenty minutes of guaranteed uninterrupted, quiet space by yourself. You may find it helpful to have a journal and pen on hand. Click the link at the end of this chapter if you'd like to listen to my audio recording of this visualisation.

Start by sitting comfortably in your chair with both your feet on the ground; feel your spine against the back of the chair and your sitting bones upon the seat of the chair. Take several deep breaths. Feel the air coming in through your nostrils and out through your mouth. As you breathe, relax your body; take this time to be present to yourself. Breathe in, breathe out. Breathe in, breathe out.

Now think of a recent situation when your toddler's behaviour registered their protest, and where you recognise you didn't handle the situation in the most helpful way. Don't judge yourself, or scold yourself. If you notice you are having a strong emotional reaction as you remember this incident, first breathe into that. Remind yourself you did the best you could at the time, and as you are more aware, you will be able to make more helpful choices in how you respond. Breathe in, breathe out. As you breathe, relax your body; be present to yourself. Breathe in, breathe out. Settle yourself. This is a time for yourself to reimagine your parenting as you'd love it to be.

As you stay in this relaxed state, we're going to look at this same situation from three different viewpoints.

1. Let's start by re-visiting the upset with your toddler through your own eyes. Imagine telling the story of the incident to a good friend, who does not judge you, or tell you what you should do. Tell your story of how the situation was for you. Notice what you are thinking and your emotional reaction. Breathe in. Breathe out. Notice the story you're telling yourself. Notice what is different when a good friend compassionately listens to you. Pause for a moment.

2. Now imagine yourself crossing the bridge so you can see the same situation from your child's perspective. Breathe in. Breathe out. Park your own emotion and your own story so you can look at this same situation through your toddler's eyes. In your imagination, shrink yourself to your child's size, so you are looking at the world, and at this incident, from your child's height and your child's ability. Imagine having your child's limited experience of life, and having only toddler vocabulary to tell you how that incident was for your child. Breathe in. Breathe out. In your imagination, hold a non-judgemental, listening space for your child. Let your gaze be soft. Relax your body so your child feels safe to share how this was for them. Listen to your toddler's story about the incident. Keep yourself on your child's side of

the bridge. Give your compassionate attention to her story, without trying to "fix it", without judgement of yourself or of your child, just listen. When your child has finished telling you their story, thank your child. In your imagination, give your child a hug, or do whatever you need to do, to reassure yourself and your child of your unconditional love. Pause for a moment.

3.   And now, in your imagination, walk onto the centre of the bridge. Stand there and quietly observe how the incident looked from your side of the bridge and how it looked from your child's perspective. Keep coming back to your breath, so you can remain in a quiet, calm, objective space. Ask yourself, "What really matters here?" And now, still standing in the centre of the bridge and holding your awareness of your child's story as well as yours, imagine how you would choose to be in a similar situation in the future. How might you handle the situation differently to help you stay in connection with your child. Or how might you handle it differently when you notice the first signs of protest? How might the situation unfold when you take an alternative approach? Imagine being on your child's side of the bridge and your child telling you their experience now. Notice how it feels inside yourself. Pause for a moment. Take a few deep breaths and when you are ready come back into the room.

Quietly reflect on any new awareness you may have, or perhaps journal this imaginary experience of crossing the bridge into your child's world.

If you would like to use my audio recording of this visualisation, click to the "Baby and Toddler Resources" private webpage for readers:

https://www.koemba.com/baby-and-toddler-resources/

In our next section we'll look at the third insight that can help us to meet the needs of a toddler. But first let's think about crossing the bridge to your baby.

29.

Cross the Bridge to
Your Baby

I am so much more aware of little Anna's alertness to her environment, and the signals she is giving, than I was with my own children at this very early age. When my own children were babies, those first smiles were brilliant, but I looked forward to them becoming toddlers, when I'd be able to communicate with them. It never occurred to me my infant child and I were *already communicating*. Because I didn't realise this, I missed some of the joy of a young infant! I knew a cry meant my child needed my help, but I didn't recognise all the wonderful little nuances of human exchange with an infant. I was a loving mother who soothed her baby when he cried, fed him when he was hungry, burped him or changed his nappy when he was uncomfortable, settled him to sleep when he needed a nap, but I did not know or understand how to cross the bridge. It was as though I was observing from the other side of a bridge. Now I'm aware of crossing the bridge - of seeing life from the child's perspective. My on-going learning in what children need to thrive has helped me to become more attuned to the child's inner world.

Notice what your baby is communicating

Anna's relaxed state of her body, or a tension, her eye movements, the turn of her head, the reaching with her hands and arms, her stretching and nuzzling, her sighs and snuffles and cries are already an amazing palette of signals, communicating with her caregivers. This little person extends an open invitation to build a bridge, that will become wider and stronger over time, and will connect her world to ours. Later she'll develop verbal skills and awareness of us as separate people to herself, but at this early stage, it's our job to create the solid foundation for that communication. Loving, connected, two-way interactions happen naturally and easily, right from this early stage, if we consistently cross the bridge. Crossing the bridge to your baby means choosing to mentally reposition yourself, so you can gain a sense of how life is from your infant's point of view.

Consistently and compassionately connect with your baby

The exciting developments in neuroscience help us understand what is happening within the baby's brain. What we now know is the part of the brain that processes emotion is already well-formed, even though the frontal cortex is still developing after birth. This means the baby does not have a verbal language yet, so they can't name emotions but, at a non-verbal level, they experience emotion and share in a mutual exchange in relationships. Babies feel emotion and need consistent connection with a loving caregiver, who mirrors those emotions. At times a baby's cry is all they have to communicate what they need. I think future generations will look back in horror that some "experts" advocated letting your baby "cry it out". Your baby is not being naughty or trying to control you - the baby's brain is not yet formed enough to develop tactics like that! Their cries and gurgles, their facial expressions and gestures are the only language they have to communicate with us. And when we don't respond to their needs there must be a terrifying sense of helplessness. When you lovingly hold your upset baby, your calm provides the much-needed soothing. Consistent, attuned connection, together with nutritionally-satisfying feeding, is what builds a healthy brain. So this is key: your baby relies on you for physical and emotional equilibrium.

Tune in to your baby's experience

When we cross the bridge the child is not left in an anxious state of alone-ness but receives a sense of, "We are together in this." They experience connectedness. This matters particularly at times when your baby is stressed or unhappy, and also when they are feeling relaxed and content, or excited. Like all of us, babies are at times contented, upset or fretful. As with the toddler, we need to parent in a way that recognises emotions aren't wrong or unwelcome - they are an expression of the child's experience. When we cross the bridge, our tone of voice, our body language and our facial expression, as well as our words, are in tune with the child's experience.

Mirror your baby's communications

It's important for the child, especially when a situation feels overwhelming, for you to mirror their experience. As you notice your baby's reactions and follow your baby's lead, you can express this:

"Aah, you're feeling sleepy after that good meal."

"Oh, you're feeling cranky."

"*That* feels good!"

Of course, the baby doesn't yet understand your words, but she senses your connection with her experience. Your rate of speech resonates with her energy level, the lilt, strength and tone of your voice, your facial expression and body language, the energy you emit; all of these can convey, "I see you. I'm sensing what you are experiencing."

We all know the expression "a picture is worth a thousand words" - well, you're the baby's mirror. You are their picture worth more than a thousand words - a wonderful, animated 3D picture!

Be your baby's emotional regulator

And crossing the bridge says "I'm here with you. It's okay, I've got a handle on it." You are your young child's emotional regulator. We, as carers, need to be present to ourselves and regulate our own emotions because our calm connectedness restores the baby's physical and emotional equilibrium. As we seek to understand how life is for the baby and what they might be experiencing, we are giving the young child a sense of self within this world. What an awesome privilege for us.

Before finishing this section, a word to the parent who is reading this and perhaps feeling upset they didn't have this knowledge with their first-born. Another exciting find from neuroscience is that the brain is able to create new pathways. When we respond empathetically to our children, we help develop their healthy brains (and ours!) to think clearly and interact compassionately. It's never too late to be the parent we want to be. So, holding both your baby and your toddler in mind, let's take a quick review of how to cross the bridge.

30.

Cross the Bridge - Recap

Often children act out because they are frustrated. When we are focused on our own agenda, we forget how the situation might be from the child's perspective.

In this section we've looked at crossing the bridge as we seek to see life as the child sees it. Often this awareness leads us to a more helpful approach, particularly at times when a child might feel overwhelmed or unseen; this is when challenging behaviours might arise. We've chatted about the importance of giving choices and being present to the child's emotional experience. We've also reflected on how to support the child when other adults don't cross the bridge. When you cross the bridge you become attuned to the child's experience and what's needed for your child and your relationship to thrive.

Of course, none of us handle our actions the way we want all the time. That's part of being human. But it does help to remember that when we're tempted to yell at each other, or trying to impose control, and things aren't working, it's not so much about the child misbehaving but because we haven't crossed the bridge. We're on opposite sides instead of being in a place of connection. When we follow the child's lead and cross the bridge we become aware of the child's perspective. It's our responsibility - response-ability! - as parents to create the connection.

In our third step we look at how we do this — what it means to "Hearth Your Home" and why this matters to create happier homes where everyone thrives.

SECTION C

HEARTH YOUR HOME

Mothering is our first preverbal template for an existence in which we feel welcomed or rejected, loved or abandoned.
Geneen Roth

My father didn't tell me how to live; he lived, and let me watch him do it.
Clarence Budinton Kelland

31.

Hearth Your Home - Introduction

In this third section, we'll explore how to create a home with "hearth" - a warm, inviting, space where family members feel safe and connected; a place where you and your children can thrive. Imagine a cosy hearth, the centre of the home where traditionally food was cooked, bread baked and coffee brewed. Throughout history, the hearth is where family and friends have gathered to warm themselves, to connect and to restore themselves. Compare that with the hob on the cooker, or the microwave, which has replaced the hearth, where we now heat our food. The slow comfort of hearth has been replaced by hurry. And that hurry often creates an atmosphere of stress. We can't turn the clock back, but we can create a home with hearth; a place where we want to gather and where we feel safe and at peace, connected and nurtured. We all need a home where there is ambience and wellbeing.

In this section, we'll chat about "hearthing" the home and how to:

- lay a foundation of relationship and trust

- ensure emotional safety

- contain big emotions when they threaten to overwhelm

- help the child to build an emotional vocabulary
- support the child to develop a coherent narrative of their life experience
- keep the child safe enough without keeping them "too safe".

When you create fabulous memory-making moments, which warm your hearts, you create a "home with hearth". Let's reflect on how this looks with Liam and his family.

32.

Naming Happy Emotions

We're sitting in the kitchen. The aroma of fresh coffee fills the room. Sophia and I share an amusing tale. We laugh. Liam looks at us, pauses for a moment and then says, "Happy."

"Yes, We're happy. We're laughing together."

We sit in comfortable silence as he plays with his blocks. My mind mulls over the brief interaction which has just occurred.

He is putting words on experiences, including happy emotions. As he articulates an abstract concept, he comprehends; he makes sense of it.

"Happy!"

His ability to articulate his inner experiences, and ours, matters because our human emotions are our inborn compass to navigate relationships. They guide us to empathise with and respond compassionately to others.

Not every experience in toddler-dom is a happy one, but we can put words to the child's experience, upsetting ones as well as happy ones, as happened with Liam the next day.

33

How to Help Your Toddler Deal with Upsets

What to do with a high-energy toddler? Especially when mum is in the late stages of pregnancy.

We've been at home all morning while workmen fixed a plumbing problem. This afternoon we need an outing.

"Do you want to wear your blue shoes or your red shoes?" Liam chooses his red shoes. Their canvas sides are elasticised and they slip on easily.

We walk past the children at play in the local schoolyard, and alongside the train track.

"Red train! Red train!" The commuter train rumbles by.

We wait for the green man on the traffic light then we cross the road.

"The yellow bus is coming soon. We must look for two-three-O."

"Lello bus, lello bus!" Liam exclaims, as a bus comes into view.

"Yes. It's a yellow bus. But it's not 2-3-0. Look. Its number is 3-0-5. Our bus is coming soon. We must look for the 2-3-0 yellow bus."

Soon Yellow Bus 2-3-0 appears.

Boarding a bus with a pushchair isn't one of my star accomplishments. My sons were raised in Africa, where the overloaded buses were a cartoonist's delight. The ancient buses were loaded beyond belief with sacks of grain, bundles of firewood, scruffy, startled hens in crude cages of bent sticks woven together and secured with wire, as more shouting and laughing people squeezed on board than you would imagine possible. If you dared to travel by public transport in rural Africa, the pushchair would have been slung on the over-piled roof-rack and your child would be in your arms.

"Backwards. Backwards," Sophia guides me as we disembark. Another parent with a pushchair gets off before me. *Aha - that's how it's done!* I have never noticed the art of navigating a pushchair off a bus until I am the one holding the handles.

It gets more complicated when we buy takeaway coffee. Liam is oblivious to the parting sea of pedestrians before us, as, head down, he pushes the chair at toddler flat-out speed. My latte spatters over my handbag as I struggle to steer us to the park.

A stretch of lawn lies between us and ducks cruise the small lake, as they wait for their handout of stale bread. Liam is off to explore. I abandon the pushchair to Sophia so I can catch up with him. He is heading for a concrete trough, only about a foot high. Its surface has a bright green carpet. *Duckweed!*

"Liam!" I call. He clambers onto the edge and steps onto the duckweed. *He thinks it's a solid surface!* His foot plunges through the film of bright green into the cold water below. He roars with fright. What he thought was a solid surface has morphed into an unexpected soaking. He's crying and won't let me touch him.

"Mama!" he roars.

Sophia holds him close. As he calms, we give him words to help him understand what's happened.

"You thought you could walk there. You didn't know there was water underneath."

The day is dry and warm enough to take his shoes off and let him run barefoot on the smooth lawn. Sophia has a raisin bun for him.

Liam eats the raisins one by one and shares the bread with the ducks quacking by his ankles. This was an unexpected adventure for him. What matters is to give the empathetic support he needs and, as he calms, to give the words to help him understand what happened.

I might have handled the situation in less helpful ways. I might have stopped him before he stepped into the water, if I'd been closer - but I would have deprived him of an important learning experience about life - things aren't always what they seem.

Another parent might have said,

"Be a big boy now. You don't need to cry."

But the tears we cry when we're upset contain stress hormones, so having a "good cry" can release the stress and as the child calms he will be more able to make sense of the situation. Strange and scary things sometimes happen in toddler-dom and life can seem dark in those moments.

Think of a Persian carpet. Its design wouldn't be so rich and attractive without the dark threads skilfully woven into the fabric. We need to help the child untangle the knots and tangles of their experience and to use words to weave them into the fabric of their lives.

The fabric of the child's life is interwoven when there is emotional safety — when they experience the support to process those experiences. How we handle upsetting incidents makes the difference; including situations that raise our own anxiety, like the one I faced the next day.

34.

How Safe Is Safe Enough?

I walk into the bathroom and my heart drops. My 22 month-old grandson is perched on top the counter with his feet in the basin. The water gushes from the taps and splashes onto the counter. He's washing his feet - an unforgiving tile floor below. The counter surface is wet. *If he falls…!* My imagination wildly pictures a broken arm or worse if he slips off this high, wet surface. I assess. He's sitting solidly. *Be calm.* I move next to him and stand there while he washes his feet. When he's ready, I offer to lift him down. Together we dry his feet, sitting on the floor.

How much to let a child explore and find out for himself? At what point do you need to take action to keep him safe?

Liam stars at the candle in the centre of the able, climbs on the chair and stretches his finger towards it.

"Hot," warns Sophia.

I catch my breath as I watch his soft little finger test the boundary. Sophia stands there - close enough to step in if the situation became dangerous. She watches. He leans closer, inching his finger towards the enticing flame. "Hot!" she repeats.

"'Ow!' He whimpers and draws back, shaking his little hand up and down as he feels the burn.

Sophia's arms fold around him. Her soft gaze meets his eyes. "Yes, the candle is hot."

Liam wasn't in danger - but close enough to the flame for it to hurt. He got the message. Fire is hot! He learns about the predictability of natural elements. The world is a safer place, physically and psychologically, when we understand its predictability.

He knows hot means hot! An anxious parent might have stopped the child — might have lifted the candle out of the toddler's reach. It takes mindful parenting to assess if the level of danger is acceptable, to contain your own anxiety without underestimating the danger, to frame the warning and yet to allow children to test for themselves. Then to stay compassionately and non-judgementally present to the child if they become upset. This matters because people, and especially children, don't learn by words alone; they need experiences to relate to that context.

Where it's safe to do so, Sophia and Alwyn let Liam find his own limits. They support him to develop understanding. They guide his actions enough to keep him from significant harm but give him enough freedom to explore. They figure the odd bruise and scrape are part of the territory of healthy toddlerhood.

Each situation needs to be assessed. Sophia sits on the far side of the kitchen table, preparing the vegetables for supper, when Liam grabs a kitchen knife.

"Mama!"

He wants to take the knife to his mother.

This isn't a butter knife. This is a kitchen knife. My ever-alert keep-him-safe teacher mode kicks in. But I know Sophia operates from the mode of trusting his competence.

What am I going to do? If I don't let him take the knife, he'll be upset. I would give him a message I don't think he's capable.

"Let me help you."

Together we carry the knife to his mother.

Later Sophia comments, "I liked the way you handled that."

Yeah, it felt the helpful thing to do; I contained my anxiety. If I'd taken the knife from him I would have given him a message,

"You are not able to do this."

This way I kept him safe while still following his lead, one step behind. But only you can decide where you need to set a boundary to keep your child safe.

For many parents, the limit here is,

"Sharp knives are for grown ups."

The situation with each child in each situation is different and needs wise, alert parenting.

No home is perfectly toddler-proof. But a too-safe environment is like a bubble-wrap that stifles the child. There is a fine line between keeping the environment safe, yet interesting and stimulating for the young child to explore. They need to test their boundaries and develop their competence, which increases their ability to keep themselves safe in other similar situations and their confidence to handle everyday situations.

If we don't keep adequate boundaries, a child could face a traumatic or painful situation, which could damage their sense of the world as a safe place. If we are over-anxious, the child may get the message this world is not a good place — it is not to be trusted. If we don't let them learn how to handle situations, they won't develop the skills they need for later life. Parenting is a constant assessment of what's needed to keep the child safe enough whilst letting them explore and develop their competence. It's a fine balance to raise children who embrace the joys and the challenges of life. That's simple enough to say - but to contain my imaginations of what might go wrong in a learning moment isn't always easy. Next day's trip to the park was a test for me to keep the balance between allowing him to test his own capabilities, whilst keeping him safe enough.

35.

Letting Your Toddler Test His Own Limits

Today Sophia's friends have planned to meet in the local park. Alwyn will drive Liam and I there and bring Sophia later so her friends can meet the baby.

Sophia asked me to put Liam's rain boots on. I was surprised - the sky was clear, no sign of rain. Why rain boots? She was right. The lawn is wet with a heavy dew. The toddlers don't mind the damp; they're playing on the swings, climbing frames and digging in a large sandpit. The grown-ups enjoy home-made bread rolls and hot coffee while we watch the children and catch up with each other's news.

A couple of the mums take their sons to see the hens. One of the boys has left his balance-bike and helmet nearby. Liam clambers onto the bike and heads for a small hill. "Hill" is an exaggeration. It's more a large mound of earth with a path cut through the long grass to a picnic table at the top. The mound isn't high, but the slope is significant for a toddler.

Up is fine. Slow - negotiable. Then he turns the bike round. I assess.

Pretty steep for a beginner. Could he fall? It's likely. Will he get hurt? Not likely - no stones or hard objects. He can't pick up too much speed on this slope. He'll fall on soft grass. Would his parents let him do this? Yes.

I stand near the base and watch. He launches. Slow at first. His speed increases. The bike wobbles. His lips purse; his eyes fixed on the path. He skims past me. Wobble. *He's going to fall!* Wobble. Wobble. He steadies the bike. The ground is levelling. He slows. He puts his feet out to the sides. He stops. He looks at me and grins.

"You came down the big slope. You went fast! You wobbled! And you stopped the bike yourself." I narrate his experience.

He turns the balance-bike around. I stop him halfway up the slope and persuade him to start from that point, so he won't be able to pick up as much speed. He launches. Whizzes to the bottom.

"Fun!" He grins at me and turns back up the hill.

I can't persuade him to stop at the halfway point. He insists on going to the top of the mound. He wants the challenge.

Would his parents let him do this? —Yes.

He pushes off. The bike picks up speed. His hands lock on the handle grips. Eyes focused on the path.

He's going fast. Too fast.

I want to call, "Be careful!" I don't. I keep quiet. I contain my anxiety.

I don't want to distract his attention from the task.

The bike's little wheels are whizzing. *Can he control it?* Slight wobble. He veers. Wobble. Wobble. His mouth opens - his bottom lip protrudes. His eyes widen.

The bike veers one way. He overcorrects. Veers in the other direction. Crash. *He's down!*

I run to him. He rolls into my arms, sobbing.

No blood. No sign of physical damage.

"You came down the big hill on the bike. You rode so fast you crashed. Oh. You fell in the grass!"

I hold him until he's ready to move. His sobs subside.

"You came down the big hill! Do you want to do it again?"

He sighs. He sits a while longer then gets up and takes the bike halfway up the hill. He doesn't look at me. He's focused on the slope before him.

He's off. He whizzes past me and comes to an easy stop.

"Again?"

He points towards the other boys who are playing on the swings again. He walks holding my hand. I carry the bike.

When we are over-protective with our children the message they may receive is this world is a dangerous place. When we're over-anxious to keep them physically safe, we overlook the potentially damaging psychological messages we may give:

"You are not capable of keeping yourself safe. You don't know how to do this. You're not competent."

It's a challenge to be a calm, contained parent when the over-anxious society we live in bombards us with messages to keep our children from bumps or bruises at all costs. But at what cost to our children's ultimate development?

It's a fine-tuned balancing act to keep a toddler safe enough but not too safe; to let them test their own capabilities. We won't be able to do this if we haven't learnt to contain our own anxiety. We need to believe in our children's capability. They develop competence by exploring; by doing.

But containing my anxiety isn't always easy…

36.

Containing Your Own Anxiety - The Challenge

Alwyn comes home from work early today. It's a golden evening. Sophia and I are suffering from a mild dose of cabin-fever and we decide to take a drive in the forest.

In a few kilometres a narrow road weaves us between tall trees. The sun's long golden shafts are broken by the diagonal shadows of the tree trunks. We stop by the main gate of the nature reserve.

Alwyn and Sophia decide the open space in the park will be a good place for Liam to ride his balance-bike. Helmet strapped on, he scoots ahead of us. The road is wide and the surface even. The open land undulates; a gentle uphill in front of us. There is little chance of a vehicle on this internal park road, and we would see it coming. This is a great place for a toddler to test his riding skills.

Oh, he scoots fast. He's so far ahead! I glance at his parents. They are strolling along, chatting to each other. *They trust him to handle this.* We've walked at least half a mile and the sun's warmth is fading when they decide to head back.

"Liam, we're going home now."

He comes to a teetering stop. He points to the road ahead. "You want to go further. We're going home now. Come this way."

Liam turns and scoots towards us. Soon he's caught up and overtakes us. He's on the downhill. There's enough of a slope to propel him. He keeps his legs up and glides forward, with ever-increasing speed. It's a gentle downhill, but the further he goes the faster his momentum. *He's far ahead of us.* A woman on a bike whizzes past us, towards my grandson. *She's so close to Liam!* He rides in the centre of the road. *What if he swerves?* I imagine a Tour de France style dramatic collision, with tumbling bodies and mangled bicycles. She cycles towards him. My heart races. My throat is strangled. I battle to swallow.

She's near him now. She slows a little. He keeps centre path. She gives him a wide berth. Away she speeds. My breath releases. *Wheew!*

I glance at my son and daughter-in-law, strolling hand-in-hand alongside me. It seems I'm the only one who's anxious. This is Denmark - a land of cyclists. These are a people who raise children to ride on public roads from an early age.

Alwyn and Sophia trust their son to handle this. *He's way ahead of us.* I am tempted to call and tell him to stop, but they are the parents. They think he's okay. And if I do call, I might break his focus. Then he could tumble. I need to contain my anxiety. My eyes fix on the little figure hurtling away from us. He gets a wheel wobble. His distant little body sways. He's going to fall! I swallow hard. We won't be there in time! I watch. Wobble. Wobble. His feet are down. Still wobbling. He's slowing himself. His scooter is off the road and into the grass. He stops, his hands grip the handles. Still upright. He looks back at us and gives a cheeky grin.

If we were closer I'm sure I'd hear him say, "Fun."

It wasn't easy to contain my anxiety. Claws scragged my throat as I watched him scoot his push-bike, way ahead of us. Tonight I check the word "anxious" in the dictionary. "Anxious" is from Latin "anxius"' - from "angere" - "to choke". Anxiety is choking! How much does our parental anxiety choke our relationship with our children? How much does our anxiety choke our child's relationship with the fascinating world they want to explore?

What's needed to contain our anxiety? It starts with being mindful. Being aware, as parents, of our own emotion. We need to name and claim our anxiety if we want to tame it. Either our anxiety is in charge of us - and our actions - or we are in charge of it. When we tame our anxiety we can respond in a helpful way which allows our child, and our relationship, to flourish. Containing our own anxiety is as essential to creating a hearthed home as yeast is to bread.

Giving hearth to your home doesn't happen by chance. It is consciously created. The next day I was given a sneak peek inside a home with hearth, where mutual respect, ambience and contentment filled the atmosphere.

37.

A Peek Inside a "Home With Hearth"

Today we are invited to Mimu's second birthday celebration. Alwyn will drop Liam and me; then he can bring Sophia and baby Anna later in the morning.

When we arrive, Liam makes a bee-line for the large plastic sit-in-and-drive car on the lawn. As he clambers in I look around. A child-friendly garden. There's a trampoline, a large bouncing horse, a scooter, sandpit, large grassy areas for children to run. I notice bicycles propped in the shed. This isn't a manicured show garden. It's a played-in garden.

Mimu's mother, Piret, invites us to a table in the garden, adorned with a small Danish flag, colourful snacks and a jug of water. *Mmmm* - the warm smell of freshly-made sourdough rolls. Pretty slices of red, yellow and orange peppers, cherry tomatoes and sliced grapes. Cubes of cheese. No sweets. No gooey cake. Sugar-free! A healthy birthday party! The children chatter as they eat. They pour drinks for themselves. A china jug! Montessori influence here. Children are trusted to be competent - able to do things for themselves.

Liam moves from eating, to swinging, to eating, to playing in the plastic car, to driving the tipper truck. Piret invites us inside. She has warm food prepared. I walk in the door and gasp with surprise. It's a comfortable space designed for family but I have never seen a sitting room like this. It gives me a sense of a family living room integrated with a well-organised Nursery School play-room. There's a TV on the wall, comfortable sofas, a coffee table with books. Not showy coffee table books, but slightly scuffed, "being read" books. The layout of the room fascinates me. I walk slowly to take it all in. The area has been structured into specific play areas. A roadmap rug is on the floor with toy cars parked on a low shelf. Plastic containers hold toy farm animals. A map of the world hangs above a 'kitchen area' with child-size units, pots and pans, implements, and dressing-up clothes hanging on a rack. A child is busy with Lego blocks. Transparent plastic containers under the counter hold other construction toys.

This isn't a toddler-only zone. This is a living room, arranged to meet every family member's needs. There are toddler toys on the lowest shelves, more advanced toys on the middle shelves and teenage gadgets on the top shelves. It isn't picture-perfect tidy. But it's not a chaotic mess of toys. There's a place for everything and everything in its place - more or less! It's a lived-in, used-and-enjoyed space for the whole family.

And good coffee! After a snack, Piret invites the children to help her pick blackberries for the cake. Liam and I walk with her to the bottom, wild end of the garden. The blackberries grow in a glorious tangle along the fence. I smile to myself. Most urban parents in Ireland or UK would think blackberries too unkempt to belong in their gardens. This isn't a garden to be admired. It's a garden is to be experienced. The toddlers harvest the blackberries.

"We pick the black ones. The black ones are good to eat. Not the red ones."

A few scratches, a few purple stains are part of the adventure.

Blackberry mission accomplished, Piret sits on the lawn with several egg whisks and a large plastic bowl with cream. She calls her son - the birthday boy - to help her whip the cream. Other toddlers take turns. Little fingers dip into the cream and then into their mouths. A toddler places the whisk on the grass. The next assistant eagerly puts it back into the cream. The cat purrs and rubs itself against Piret's back. A health and safety officer would shake her head and cross the boxes. But this is the world of happy, perfectly imperfect, healthy toddler-dom.

Piret brings the single-layer homemade sponge cake to the outdoor table. The children help her to decorate it, smoothing on the thickened cream - licking the spatulas clean. They sprinkle the blackberries on top. Piret places two candles in the centre of the cake. Everyone gathers round. Piret lights the candles. Mimu blows hard. The flame wavers. Another puff. Mimu blows the candles out.

They all clap and sing the Danish birthday song. I don't know the words but I hum along. Piret slices the cake and passes it around. *Mmm.* Freshly made. Slightly sweet. Healthy food.

Alwyn and Sophia have arrived in time to celebrate with us.

I savour the experience. The adults coo over the baby. Papa pushes Liam on the swing.

This was a happy birthday. What an inviting home with hearth! A home which nurtures the child, but it isn't all about the child. It's a consciously created environment where each family member matters. A home where things don't have to be perfect. A home where anxiety will be soothed because of how we choose to be. A home where souls are warmed.

And of course, any home with a toddler has its challenging moments …

38.

Toddler Tantrums - What Helps?

From my room I can hear Liam's voice rising. His protests become louder. Sophia's voice stays calm. He roars. Sophia's voice stays calm. He wails. Sophia's voice stays calm. At last Liam's protest softens to sobs. They begin to talk again.

"You feel angry when you can't …"

Liam's parents acknowledge his feelings. They calmly ride the storm of his big emotion. No blaming. No shaming. No threatening or cajoling him to "be a good boy" or a "big boy".

They contain their own emotions and create a safe space for him. They hearth the home. And every parent knows toddlers have big emotions - big happy emotions, big sad emotions, big anxious emotions and big angry emotions. These sad, fearful or angry emotions sometimes spill over into tantrums.

Why toddler meltdowns happen

One of the key biological reasons young children tend to become frustrated and overwhelmed by strong emotions is because the brain is not yet fully formed. In the mature brain, the two hemispheres have a "highway" joining them. This is called the corpus callosum. This "highway'" has information traffic buzzing back and forth between the two. The right hemisphere handles emotions and creativity and the left hemisphere computes our logical reasoning and processes language. The toddler's corpus callosum highway isn't fully functional yet. This means the young child can't think and reason in the way we think and reason, especially in moments when they are overwhelmed.

The toddler is trying to make sense of the confusing world of words, facts, relationships, experiences, emotions - but this "highway" which integrates their brain's processing isn't yet adequately formed. The brain doesn't yet have an adequate bridge to cope with the huge volume of information traffic. Sometimes, the amount of stimulation can overwhelm the toddler's brain, causing "traffic overloads" and congestion, which lead to meltdowns.

The young child is not always reason-able - able to reason - because the brain is still developing. They are not being naughty. They're not "being a brat".

At times they get frustrated because the world feels too big to handle. And the frustration can be too big for them to contain.

The child can't find a favourite toy. They can't get you to understand what they want. The child's body experiences the turbulence of strong emotions like fear, anxiety and frustration, but they can't articulate this. It makes sense the young child will express this experience in whatever way they can - even a meltdown!

What the overwhelmed toddler needs

In fact, when we understand this we'll perceive the toddler tantrum as a natural and healthy outlet - not behaviour to be immediately stopped. When we see the situation from the child's perspective - following the child's lead and crossing the bridge - our intuition will guide us to what the child needs to process the experience.

They need support to regain their equilibrium, and then to give words to their experience, so they learn to name and understand their emotional reactions.

Because their brain is still under construction they can't yet self-regulate. In fact, at the toddler's developmental level, we have the perfect storm for a tantrum — toddlers *can't* self-regulate. They can't adequately articulate their experience, and they don't have enough life experience to understand every situation they find themselves in. They can't calm themselves. They rely on our calm to calm their strong emotions. When children are most unlovable is when they need our love the most. We are the ones whose brains have a developed processing system — we are the ones who need to model keeping calm.

When the toddler becomes overwhelmed by their own intense emotions, what they most need is for us to regulate our own emotions and to contain theirs — to non-judgementally absorb the big, overwhelming emotion till it naturally subsides. This is part of hearthing the home.

What to do if the child's upset behaviour could be dangerous

There are emergency situations, when a child's behaviour might put themselves or someone else in danger, where you need to react to ensure safety. If the child heads towards a dangerous situation, you do what you need to do to keep them safe. There are times when a big voice or a firm action might be needed to intervene when a situation could be dangerous. Afterwards when everyone is calm again, you may need to apologise and explain: "I'm sorry I shouted at you to stop. But we play in the garden, not on the road."

Containing your own reactivity

Unless it's an emergency situation, we as adults need to respond, rather than react, if we want to hearth the home. As I once heard,

"When you say you 'lost it' you mean you lost your adult-hood."

We all have moments when we lose our cool. There will be moments when we react unhelpfully, when our anxiety contaminates our behaviour and our relationships. We might give out, yell, nag or resort to controlling behaviour; we might talk where we need to listen or over-function in some other unhelpful way. In these instances, we often feel disappointed, guilty or upset with ourselves afterwards. Those emotions are our relational compass, guiding us to True North in our connection and communication. Guiding us on to how to hearth our homes.

When we are mindful to our own emotions, we can use them to guide us to what really matters. We can choose to regulate our own emotions, and regain our equilibrium so we can be there for the child and create a different outcome. The child may still have a tantrum, but we can be the emotional container they need. We can create a protective, insulation around the child's potentially explosive reaction, so there isn't serious fallout. We consciously hearth the home.

The starting point to create a different outcome is to take a few deep breaths. Breathe in - breathe out. Breathe in - breathe out. When we steady our breathing we steady our thoughts. The more we are aware, the more we can step back from the situation and ask ourselves,

"What's needed to create a win-win outcome?"

Why your self-care matters

And parents need a safe listening space themselves - a safe space to process the challenges of what it takes to be a mindful parent. When we have a hearthed place to reflect on the frustrations, challenges and joys of parenting, it's easier to contain our own big emotions and to stay connected to our child's emotional needs.

When we are emotionally connected, it doesn't mean the toddler gets to do whatever they please. Neither is it about trying to control the child - that's never possible! Rather, we are in control of our own responses. Our children need the emotional security of knowing we can handle it. Each challenge is a growth opportunity; we can create reconnection, no matter what unfolds. Rupture and repair are part of relationship. We can turn the power struggle of an "I" decision into a "we" decision. When we regulate our own emotions, we will be able to listen to our intuition and be present in a way that guides us to hearthing our home, even in the uncertain and confusing moments. Be the calm your child needs.

And hearthing the home also means having fun together.

39.

How to Get Down to the Child's Level

Alwyn is sitting on the kitchen floor. We often find ourselves on the floor now there's a toddler in the home, and the underfloor heating makes this a comfortable place to be.

Liam has been playing with his toys a short distance from his dad and now he looks at him.

"Come on — rugby dive!"

Liam's face breaks into a big grin. He launches himself at his dad. Alwyn's arms stretch out to catch the little body hurtling towards him. They laugh and hug. Then Alwyn sets him on his feet again.

Liam moves about four foot of way from his dad and again launches himself full force at his dad. Laughs and hugs - back on his feet. Again and again he runs, he launches, his dad catches him; laughs and hugs, ready for the next assault. Dad and son's eyes twinkle. Grinning. Focused on each other.

We hearth the home when we have fun together. We play together. The family who plays together stays together. This makes sense because when we have fun our bodies release endorphins - feel-good chemicals - which dampen the cortisol stress levels. When cortisol levels lower, there is less reactive behaviour, so there's less stress, and, when there is less stress, then less cortisol will be produced. We ease the stress when we have more fun in the family. Families who have fun together laugh more and relax more. And there's less sibling rivalry.

To hearth the home we need to come alongside the child in play opportunities and get down to the child's level at times of upset. Get down to the child's level not only physically but also cross the bridge to see the situation through the child's eyes. Yesterday I was out with Liam when I noticed a young girl in the adjoining school playground. She stood with her fingers gripping the triangles of the fence; she stared at the ground, her back to the school and all the children. One of the staff came to her. He knelt beside her, his hand also holding the fence. He was close to her but did not invade her space. He spoke to her - she shook her head. He waited - watching her; giving her time. A few minutes later he spoke to her again. This time she shook her head, still looking down, but she said a word or two to him. He nodded. He waited. A few moments and she said a few words. This time she glanced at him. It took another five or ten minutes. He stayed engaged. He did not hurry her. I couldn't hear the conversation but the body language, the timing, painted a picture. He gave her space. He was in tune with her. He made it safe for her to share her story. He didn't try to hurry the process. He was present to her. He was at her level.

By the time Liam and I leave, the child and the teacher were both peddaling around the playground on the large carts. (Yes, you read me right, the teacher was riding a cart too! It's the strong who can afford to be weak.)

Denmark is often voted the happiest country in Europe. Is this because they take time to connect with their children's experience? Is this because they hearth their homes? The Danes use the word "hygge" - pronounced hue-gah - *"a feeling or mood that comes from taking genuine pleasure in making ordinary everyday things simply extraordinary."* **Alex Beauchamp**

That night as I journal, I wonder if the Danes have gained some insight into child-raising that many of us have missed. What is the secret they know?

40.

Is Your Child Naughty?

I'm the last out the door and the family is already in the car.

My adult son teasingly eases the car forward, as though he'll leave me behind. I jump into the back seat with a smile,

"Oh, you're naughty!"

"Naughty," repeats my toddler grandson.

"That's a word he's never heard before!" says his mother.

As we travel I muse how much I appreciate that his parents never label him as "naughty". They never refer to him as a "bold child", even at times when he's acting out. When his behaviour is challenging, they are aware there's something going on for him that needs attention. They never perceive him as being naughty!

Isn't it strange, We never use the word "naughty" to describe an adult, unless we say "He has a naughty sense of humour," or "naughty underwear". As we wait in the traffic queue, this thought intrigues me. We give "naughty" a different meaning for adults. When we talk about a child being naughty, we mean, "This child won't do what he's told. The child won't comply." In other words, we're saying, "My child won't follow my agenda." But when a child chooses to follow his own path, not ours, it doesn't mean he's "naughty" - or "bold" as we'd say in

Ireland. The child who walks to the beat of a different drum is often the one who, as an adult, is most likely to make a significant difference in the world - think Steve Jobs, Richard Branson, actor Robin Williams.

"Do you have a word in Danish for 'naughty?'" I ask Sophia.

"No, not really," she says. "If we are talking about a child who is often acting out we might comment the child is, 'Uopdragen. 'Opdrage' means, 'to raise'. So 'uopdragen' literally means 'unraised'."

Interesting! "'Uopdragen" is not saying the child is naughty — it is not shaming the child. It is not making the child "wrong". It is saying the parent hasn't fulfilled the responsibility of raising the child — the parent hasn't given the child the support and skills needed to interact successfully. I think the Danish expression is significant because it emphasises it is our job as parents to raise our children. And yes, it can be a very challenging task.

To "opdrage" - to raise your child, whether your child is "easy to raise"or challenging - takes mindful parenting, commitment and consistency. Instead of labelling the child, instead of shaming or blaming them, we as adults need to respond to what each children uniquely needs. Like wise gardeners, with consistent effort and wisdom, we can raise our children to thrive - "Opdrage".

This is what hearthing our homes is about - making it safe, warm and a place of compassionate connection. Rather than manipulate the situation, we can facilitate interactions so we meet the child's need as well as our own. Hearthing the home means we and our children have a place to restore our sense of wellbeing, so they have the courage and confidence to venture into the big world.

How might this impact our children as they grow older?

41.

What We Can Learn From Danish Parenting

One of the projects I have wanted to do whilst I am here is tidy the front garden. Today I've cut the hedge and I'm sweeping the last leaves off the sidewalk when two cars park close to me. The doors open and out bounce a group of pre-teens. Healthy, energetic kids, who pick up their small backpacks and cross the road, heading towards the corner. The adults saunter behind the group, chatting together and paying no great attention to the youngsters.

As the kids near the corner, a girl stops and looks at the high wall, made of large round stones, which borders the corner property. It's at least eight foot tall. Round, smooth stones. She tilts her head back to assess the wall, her long blond hair flowing behind her. She reaches her hands to grip the stones above her. She finds her first foothold. She clambers up the rock face, shifting her hands and feet, one at a time, to seek the next crevice to rest her foot. She reaches for the next handhold. She hoists her body from stone to stone. The others stop. They watch. The girl pulls herself upright on the top of the high wall. She spread-eagles her arms in triumph. She balances along the top of the wall. A boy throws his backpack on his shoulders. Up he goes. The challenge is taken. One by one her friends clamber up the wall. The adults walk along, immersed in their conversation, unperturbed by the children's adventure. The corner intersects a much busier road, carrying residential traffic. Nobody shouts, "Be careful." You could think they haven't noticed what the children are doing, but they trust their children are capable.

I smile. This is the environment where my grandson is being raised. In my month here, I have not seen a single child with an arm in plaster, a bandaged head or on crutches. Has anyone researched whether children raised in an environment where they are encouraged to be competent suffer any more - or less! - injuries than a child raised in a more protective environment?

Does our well-intentioned interference rob our children of the opportunities to discover what works and what doesn't, what they can do and what they can't?

Perhaps we undermine their confidence. We get in the way of them learning to trust their instincts of what they can do. Perhaps, later in life, when they are in a position of having to do things independently, they won't have developed the skills they need to handle the physical or psychological challenges of life. In trying to protect our children we may create a fearful atmosphere which erodes their confidence. Perhaps our parenting would benefit from a healthy bucketful of Danish mentality.

I lie in my bed that evening - staring at the ceiling. *Clackety-clack, clackety-clack* - the train passes by. *I'll be leaving soon!* My mind sifts though the images of these past weeks. I have been impacted by the parenting culture in Denmark in an unexpected way. I've seen in action how we can build our children's physical, mental and emotional competence. I turn my light on again and pick up my pen. I need to journal this:

It is more than developing skills, confidence and response-ability. It's more significant than that! Two major transformations occur in the brain during a human life — once during toddlerhood and again during the teenage years. During these phases, a process called myelination occurs. In this massive restructuring process the unstimulated parts of the brain are pruned. If you don't use it you lose it.

Have we been duped into an over-protective parenting role which causes damaging myelination to toddlers and teens, and costs them significant brain development?

Are we robbing them of the life experiences they need to grow a mature brain?

What are children losing when we don't allow them challenging experiences? What might over-protective parenting be costing our children?

What's the price of doing everything for them? Is our over-anxious care of our children depriving them what they need to thrive?

I put my journal aside and think about my visit to the Viking Ship Museum in Roskilde. It struck me these voyagers didn't set out over wild seas to unknown destinations in blind fanaticism; rather, I perceived, it was trust in themselves and their competence. I imagined how they planned, they prepared, they took account of what they knew did and didn't work. They prepared themselves for the journey before they set out. Courage isn't the absence of fear, but the decision to act despite one's fear.

As parents we need courage, despite our fear, to step out into the unknown future to help our children, and ourselves, grow to our fullest potential. When we provide the warmth and stability of a hearthed home, we provide essential elements to encourage stamina and courage for new adventures. The hearth is the safe place to comfort and inspire us.

The warmth of the hearth depends on the commitment of the ones who keep the fire stoked. Being the protector of the hearth isn't always easy. It takes conscious decision and hard work. Let's remind ourselves of what's needed to create the sense of hearth that warms home and hearts.

42.

Tips to "Hearth Your Home" When It Isn't Easy

"Love is extending yourself to cause the other person's growth."

Scott Peck

I take this quote by Peck to mean we need to extend ourselves to live through our own uncertainties and anxieties; to learn to contain our own challenging emotions so we can hearth the home. Keeping the warmth, security, stability and ambience of the hearth well stoked, can be challenging. Here are five practical tips:

1. Recognise feelings are our relationship compass

Recognise how your own emotions can guide you to what's need, providing you don't let anger or anxiety have the steering wheel.

Model that feelings are never wrong — it's what we do with them that counts. Help your child to build an emotional vocabulary, to name and claim their emotions, by discussing emotions and weaving this into your regular speech: "You're sad we can't stay longer."

"You're happy - Thomas is safely home!"

"The baby's crying. What do you think she is trying to tell us?"

Use situations in life, in storybooks and in films to chat about feelings and how we can respond to other people's feelings.

2. Be relaxed and flexible yet keep to a routine as far as possible

Routine gives your children a sense of security. Create a child friendly environment at home, which naturally eliminates a lot of "no's"! Yet not so safe that there is little interest or challenge. Children need to test their developing abilities. Have as few rules as possible — these need to be for safety / respect of others and of property.

3. Contain your own anxiety

Your young child is discovering the amazing world in which they live.

The child needs you to contain your anxiety so you support them to grow into the fullness of their potential. They aren't yet able to contain their big emotions. They need your calm to regain their emotional equilibrium. Don't bubble-wrap, or contaminate their experience. Contain your anxiety or anger. When it's hard to be grounded, bring yourself back to your breathing and mind your thoughts.

4. Recognise "rupture and repair" is part of every relationship

Be kind to yourself. You won't handle every situation perfectly. You're human. Relationships rupture and relationships repair.

What matters is to get back on track as soon as possible. Model to your child how we repair relationship. They'll need those skills too!

5. Forgive yourself when you don't handle things the way you wanted to

It's easy as a parent to feel guilty. None of us manage our relationships the way we want to all the time.

If you handled something in a way that has left you feeling guilty, repair the relationship and figure out how to handle similar situations in a more helpful way next time. Then let go the guilt because your stressed emotion will get in the way of you being the calm, centred parent you need to be for your children to thrive.

Click this link to the"Baby and Toddler Resources" private webpage for readers, where you can download these tips:

https://www.koemba.com/baby-and-toddler-resources/

Print the page and place somewhere to remind you of key points to hearth your home, when you most need it.

Now for another experiment.

43.

YOUR EXPERIMENT - Create a Home with Hearth

Here's a brief activity to reflect on what creating a home with heart - hearthing your home - might mean for you.

When you have a quiet space, sit comfortably and take a few deep breaths to centre yourself. Now imagine a cosy, warm home with a fire blazing in the hearth. What images, what emotions, what sounds come to your mind. Notice how your body feels when you imagine relaxing at your hearth. Let yourself absorb the experience. What does this say to you about the home atmosphere you create? Take time to reflect upon this and what it means for your day-to-day parenting.

Now here's the second part of this reflection. You'll need a pen and paper for this activity.

Remember as a child taking a word and seeing how many small words you could find with the letters in that word? For example, if you took the word "Constantinople" you could find the words "constant", "instant", "top", "ant", etc.

Take a sheet of paper and write the word "hearth" at the top. Now write all the words you can find using the letters from the word "hearth"' If you do this as a written exercise it strengthens the learning experience. See how many words you can find. Reflect on the possible significance of each of the words you have written, when you think about what's needed to create a home with hearth.

Perhaps you might choose to make a poster of a hearth and these words to remind yourself of hearthing your home. A creative expression of your ideas involves the right hemisphere of you brain, as well as the left, which means when you use a hands-on approach you better retain your learning. Why not make it a family project and all get involved! I'd love you to post your pictures on social media - use these hashtags: #homewithhearth and #BabyAndToddlerOnBoard

Now let's look a hearthing the home for your baby.

44.

Hearthing the Home For Your Baby

This home, like many Danish homes, has a beautiful wood-burning stove to heat the living room on a cold day. It's functional, and it adds an emotional warmth and ambience to the room. It is the modern equivalent of a hearth; as we relax and watch the sputtering flames leap and crawl and curl in a dance of colour, which mellows the room. When we create a home with hearth - we create a warm, inviting space where all family members, including baby, feel safe and connected. Let's reflect on how to hearth the home regarding a baby's needs.

Lay a foundation of relationship and trust

Even as adults we need to sense when someone is non-judgmentally present to us, accepting who we are and how we are. Each one of us needs to be heard, to be seen, to "feel felt" and to have a sense of connectedness and belonging. Whatever our age, we subconsciously ask, "Are you with me?" We are hard-wired to flourish when we are in safe, affectionate and attuned relationship with each other. Establish your support base to ensure you have others who will share the load and help you to rest and recalibrate.

Ensure your baby's physical and emotional safety

Your baby relies on you for protection, food, stimulation and comfort. Imagine being unable to move around, unable to pick up what you want, unable to eat or drink unassisted. Because of your baby's helplessness and dependence, being separated from you, or from another familiar and warmly-connecting caregiver, is stressful for a baby.

It always concerns me when I hear a baby's distressed crying and the adult just keeps pushing the pram - out of sight and touch. The baby needs to be picked up, or at least see the caregiver's face, feel a soothing touch and hear the close, reassuring sounds of a voice they know and trust. Imagine if we saw an elderly, frail person crying out for help, and we ignored them. Yet why do we ignore the cry for help of a tiny, helpless infant! When a child is upset their body becomes flooded with stress chemicals. Neuroscientists tell us young children are not able to calm themselves. If you leave your baby to "cry it out" you are leaving their immature brain swimming in toxic stress chemicals. Yes, they may stop crying from exhaustion and hopelessness, but at what cost to their well-being?

It was a huge shock to me, when my children were already adult, to realise the potential impact of letting my baby cry - the mindset was it "was spoiling a baby" to pick them up. But crying is the baby's only way of telling us their experience and letting us know they are in need.

No matter what age our children, we can't change the past but we can do differently now.

Contain big emotions when they threaten to overwhelm

At first, your baby's cries are their only language. This is how your baby gives you cues as to what they need, and as you respond you lay the foundation for everything your little one learns about their world.

Our task as parents is to keep our babies emotionally safe, as well as physically safe. Because your baby's brain is not yet fully developed, they cannot self-regulate. They cannot calm themselves down. And your calm body co-regulates your baby's upset system. That's one reason why your self-care matters too.

Your baby needs skin-to-skin direct body-to-body contact with you, so your calm body can regulate your baby's body. Babies need to be held. Some parents leave a baby to cry, saying, "They stop eventually." Yes, they do. They stop crying from exhaustion. They abandon hope that anyone will meet their needs. Science has shown that babies who have cried themselves quiet have a high level of the toxic stress-chemical cortisol in their bodies. The baby abandons their cry for help - and feels abandoned too. Your baby may look fine, but the stress levels can be boiling inside. When you calm your distressed baby the cortisol level recedes. Your baby is entirely dependent on you to create their emotional safety.

We talked about implicit memory earlier. Your baby's repeated experience of a warm, connected and responsive relationship with you will be a resource they carry within their bodies for the rest of their lives.

Help your baby to lay a foundation for an emotional vocabulary

From a baby's very early days, they are capable of sharing their feelings with their caregivers. This emotional communication isn't an ability we "lose" when we develop a vocabulary - our non-verbal interaction remains an essential part of how we share our ideas and feelings throughout our lives. Watch any couple when you cannot hear their words, and notice how much you can determine about their interaction. How we say something is possibly more important than what we say. We chat with our babies, building their awareness of speech as a means to communicate. And let's remember we are *already communicating* with them through sounds, touch, gestures, and facial expression!

Build the foundation for your baby to develop a coherent narrative of their life experience

Notice your baby's reactions and follow your baby's lead, using words to describe the emotions you observe:

"You're sleepy."

"That was fun!"

"Oooh, you don't like that."

"You're feeling cranky tonight."

As you express your baby's inner experience and mirror with your tone, facial expression and body language, your child begins to build an awareness. That vocabulary of emotion will become a coherent narrative - an interweaving of self-worth and caring, connected interaction with others.

A word to the other parent

You may be unaware of how powerful your presence can be as a calming influence, both for mother and children. The practical things you do can be hugely helpful, in easing the load of never-ending chores: doing the housework, making a meal, minding the toddler, or minding both children so mother can rest. Sometimes you don't need to *do* anything; you just need to cross the bridge and listen to her experience without making suggestions. "Sounds like you had a tough day!" You're feeling tired?" Listen to her and reflect her experience. Ask your partner what she needs. Your presence can be the calm she needs to recalibrate herself, or, at times of family stress, maybe your role needs to be soothing the distressed toddler or the baby. At times doing nothing other than being calmly and empathetically present, without going into "fix-it" mode, might be the most helpful thing you can do. Your compassionate calm may be the most important thing you can *do* for your partner and your children.

In future years we will reap what we sow, both in our one-to-one relationships and in larger society. Gentleness, caring, empathy, understanding and respect are qualities we need in this world now, more than any time in history if there is going to be a tomorrow for our children and future generations. Let's be the difference that makes the difference.

In the next chapter we'll recap these principles, as they apply to your toddler, so we can create a mental map of how we want to parent.

45

Hearth Your Home - Recap

In this section we have looked at key aspects of what is needed to hearth your home - both regarding yourself and your child, and also the shared space in which you live together. To create comfort and security, we need to:

Lay a foundation of trust

This is not only about your child trusting you, but also about you having a sense of trust in yourself, as parent. You need a safe space to process your parenting experience, so you can be a safe space for your child, so they in turn can learn to trust themselves.

When you consistently and empathetically respond to your child you create an emotionally stable base where it's safe for your child to explore the world and to learn from experiences. This is the foundation every child needs to grow to be a caring, reflective and competent human being.

Ensure emotional safety

When you hearth your home you ditch destructive ways of expressing emotional experiences. There's no blaming, shaming or ignoring. Acknowledge your child's emotional response and affirm their experience.

"You didn't like the big dog barking at you."

"You were sad because you wanted me to come."

Contain big emotions when they threaten to overwhelm

The young child's brain is still under-construction, so it is not helpful to ignore big emotions, toddler tantrums or other behaviours linked to strong feelings. Whilst we may at times feel frustrated, the young child needs adults to contain these big emotions, so they are supported in their struggle through them.

Support your child to develop a coherent narrative of their life experience

The home with hearth is a space where experiences can be acknowledged and processed, so they can be woven into the fabric of our lives.

Your toddler needs you to acknowledge their emotions and experiences. Later when calm is restored, chat about incidents so your child can develop the vocabulary to express themselves and to make sense of their experiences.

Take time to help your child process upsetting or unfamiliar experiences.

They learn "this is how we do life".

Acknowledge their experience; chat with them about the incident, without belittling, blaming or shaming. You may find it helpful to encourage your child to draw their experience or talk about it using toys or props.

When they want to talk, listen deeply, so they can tell you their story. Give them the message, through your listening,

"I see you. I want to understand your experience."

When they can understand what happened and process the experience they will be more able to cope in similar situations next time.

Don't overprotect your child

Keep them physically and emotionally safe enough without keeping them "too safe". By hearthing the home we create the safe, heart-warming place which gives them the security, stability and courage they need to face the world.

To hearth the home we need to follow the child's lead and cross the bridge, so we can see life from the child's perspective. As I typed this, my Macbook's autocorrect changed "hearthing" to "heartening". Heartening ourselves, and our children, is what hearthing the home is all about. When home is hearthed, we as a family can step out into the amazing adventure of life. If we are serious about breaking the cycle of abuse and violence which has cursed our human race through the centuries, it won't happen because of the politicians. We have to begin in the home. We as parents are nurturing the seeds of change that will blossom in future generations. We help our children create an image of themselves as people who can make a loving difference in this world. The difference that's needed!

Keep in mind these three tenets:

* **follow your child's lead**
* **cross the bridge**
* **hearth your home**

Create your own support network, or join me online www. koemba.com, where you will find links to my social media and other resources, to give yourself the support you need, because parenting is the most important job we can ever do.

Read on for a glimpse of the last few hours before my departure.

CONCLUSION

How lucky am I to have something that makes saying goodbye so hard.
Winnie the Pooh

46.

Not Long Till Departure

Five weeks seemed a long time when I was folding my clothes, packing for my journey here.

Now I'm repacking my suitcase - a bag of dirty laundry, heavy jersey I haven't needed, old shoes scuffed from garden work, wrapped in a plastic bag.

It will be good to be in my own space again. I miss the open green behind our house and throwing ball for our dog. *Aaaaah!* It's going to be so hard to leave. I wipe the back of my sleeve over my eye.

I'm folding my blouses when Liam and Sophia come into the room. Liam squats on the floor, driving the dinky cars parked in my room. Sophia sits on the couch next to the suitcase. She and I agreed to wait until the last day before we tell Liam I am leaving.

"Liam," she says. "See, Farmor is putting her clothes in the suitcase."

Liam lines up his trucks.

"Farmor has to leave tomorrow. She's going in the aeroplane. She's going to her house."

We both watch Liam, wondering how much he will comprehend.

He leaves his toys on the floor. He cuddles in to his mother; gazes into her eyes for a moment, then says,

"Deedee."

Sophia and I both smile. Deedee is the little dog that belongs to his other grandmother. Deedee came to stay for a few months and then went home again. Liam understands.

47.

My Last Morning

I wake early. I slip out of bed. For the first time in the whole month everyone is still fast asleep when I get up. They are all together in "big, big bed".

I move into my grandson's empty bedroom, to have a cosy space to work. I nestle on the small couch and prop my Macbook on a cushion.

The scent of the cushion! I hold it against my cheek and absorb the smell. A soft milky smell, the last of his "baby scent". He is growing so fast. This is my last time with him when I will still be able to smell his babyhood.

I think of his kisses. When he chooses to give a kiss he gives it so fully. His eyes fixed on my face, his whole body comes in for the kiss. A coming-to-kiss-you kiss. A full-on whole body, here-I-am-kissing-you kiss. A fully present-to-the-moment toddler kiss. Total giving. Like everything else he does in his toddler way, he kisses with his full attention.

I sigh. The sweet smell of the cushion is in my nostrils.

Little things. Magic things. Things I never consciously noticed with my own children.

I feel a tear roll down my cheek. Only hours till I leave.

Afterword

"The ultimate lesson all of us have to learn is unconditional love, which includes not only others but ourselves as well."

Elisabeth Kubler-Ross

The thoughts I've shared about what children need to thrive might make you feel concerned there have been times when you haven't "been there" for your child in the way you know your child needed you, so here are three important things to remind yourself:

- No parent parents perfectly all the time. Be kind to yourself and get the support you need because parenting isn't meant to be a solo job. Through all of history parenting has been a community responsibility.

- Neuroscience tells us the brain is "plastic", meaning it continues to grow and change. Rather than going on a guilt-trip on what you did or didn't do yesterday, that you can't change, use this information and your intuition to guide you to how you choose to parent *now*! And be gentle with yourself. This is a huge transition for you too.

- You are taking time to read this book because you're serious about being the parent you want to be!

As we know better we do better. Wishing you a joyful home, filled with wonderful discoveries about life, about yourself and about the precious members of your family. Read on if you are looking for practical resources to implement what we've been chatting about.

APPENDICES

APPENDIX 1

Coping With Baby And Toddler - Practical Tips

Maybe you don't have someone who can move in to help. Maybe your partner can't take leave. Maybe you are a single parent. Or if you parent alone, even for part of the day, here are insights and tips you may find helpful, because calmly navigating the tough moments will help you guide your family through this transition.

- In the weeks before baby's birth, collect simple toys and interesting books to have available when needed for your toddler. Watch flea markets and charity shops for bargain prices of quality toys.

- Have a bag of toys that are "new" to your child to use at times when your child needs to be entertained.

- Accept the help offered. If people ask how they can help, tell them what would be helpful: to run an errand, take the toddler out for a while, clear the dishes at the sink, deliver a meal. Friends and family often want to help - but they aren't sure how. Tell them what you need. Perhaps write a short list so you don't have to think about it when asked.

- You might not manage nutritionally balanced meals every meal. Think about achieving balance through the week, rather than worrying about a particular meal. It's as easy to buy fruit and quality yoghurt as junk food! Batch cook so you have tomorrow's meal sorted as well as today's. A slow cooker can be a great investment. Use online shopping to purchase your groceries — ideally, organise this several weeks before baby's birth so you have a handle on this before life becomes baby-focused.

- Invest in a baby sling, so you can freely move around.

- Involve your toddler in helping. Store baby's nappies etc. at a height your toddler can reach, to bring to you. Your child will likely be more co-operative if they see themselves as team members.

- When the baby sleeps, enjoy special time with your toddler: cuddle up together for a nap, read a book together, draw, or have fun with play-dough (a great stress reliever). Your toddler needs quality time with you.

- Nap when you have the opportunity! No mother is ever remembered for her perfect ironing. You'll be more able to handle things well when you have enough sleep. Look after yourself so you can look after them.

- Favourite nursery rhymes or similar on the iPad or TV might give you a break when you desperately need it. But be mindful of limiting total screen time to no more than an hour a day at this stage of your child's development.

- Use baby's feeding time and other opportunities to read stories or chat with your toddler, so they are included too.

- Baby needs you to coo and smile and interact - but baby isn't worried about what you're saying. So chat to baby about her awesome big brother, or sister. Tell baby all the things you love about your toddler, and what you and your toddler do together. You are giving attention to baby, and you are reassuring your child they are also loved and valued.

- Create a routine as best you can. It will be worth it because they cope better when there is a natural rhythm to their day. Try to walk every day. Your toddler is more likely to cooperate when they can burn off energy and enjoy the stimulation of seeing things outside the four walls of home. And it's good for you too! Have a tote bag prepared with what you need for an outing for baby and toddler - and for yourself - so it's easy to grab and go when the opportunity arises.

- In stressful moments, rather than giving out to your toddler or holding the tension inside yourself, choose to calm yourself. At times when you feel like you are going to lose your cool, focus on your breathing. Take several deep breaths and each time exhale fully through your mouth. When you steady your breathing you steady your thoughts. Young children's brains are not developed enough for them to emotionally regulate themselves. Your stress will only increase their stress and you will all end up on the stressed-out merry-go-round. Your toddler relies on your calm to restore their equilibrium.

- When you have steadied your breathing, observe your thoughts. Often our thoughts stress us out. *"I can't take any more of this.—I can't cope."* When you adjust your thoughts, you can lower your stress. If a negative thought pops into your head, re-angle it. Reword your thought.

Rather than thinking "I can't take this", change that to, "It's hard to cop*e right now.*"

Rather than thinking, "We can't get into a routine", reword your thought: "We haven't established a routine *yet.*"

Choose thoughts which remind you there's light at the end of the tunnel. Avoid words like "can't", "never"and "always" - they dim your vision of how things could be. Notice whether your thoughts are helpful or whether they are increasing your stress. Change your words and you will change your perspective. Change your perspective and you lower your anxiety. You'll be able to think more clearly about what's needed and what you *can* do.

- Strive to see life from your toddler's perspective. This addition to the family is a huge change for your child as well as for you. Your toddler had no idea life was going to be turned upside down!

- Take time for fun. Fun releases endorphins - feel good chemicals. And endorphins dampen the cortisol stress levels. The positive effect of fun-times reduces the impact of the stress-times.

- Know home won't be "perfect" for the weeks ahead. Adjust your expectations. Don't add stress you don't need. Be kind to yourself and to your family. When things feel overwhelming remember, "This too will pass." If you're feeling overwhelmed, ask for help. You can't pour from an empty cup. Get the help you need for your family's sake, as well as your own.

- Choose gratitude rather than self-criticism. When you look around you and see disarray, instead of saying to yourself, "What a mess!" smile and focus on being thankful for your family.

Click this link for your downloadable page of these tips, so you can print it off and place somewhere to remind you of being the parent you want to be, when you might most need it.

https://www.koemba.com/baby-and-toddler-resources/

On the next page you'll find a note to those supporting a baby and toddler family.

APPENDIX 2

A Note to Those Supporting a Baby and Toddler Family

As someone who wants to support, it isn't always easy to figure out what's helpful. Here are suggestions, but trust your own wisdom to figure out what's needed in the particular situation you find yourself.

Instead of saying, "Give a shout if you need help," just do it!

Check what time is good for a visit, so you don't arrive when they have managed to catch a nap.

Arrive with a yummy treat. Perhaps they would like you to stay and share it with the family, but make it clear you are also happy for them to keep it till later if they would prefer.

Arrive with a prepared meal. Or give a voucher for a take-away meal.

Deliver a bag of handy groceries. And include a treat!

If the children are comfortable with you, ask if you can take the toddler or the baby - or both - for a walk.

Ask if you can take the toddler out to play. Only take the child on an outing if the child is happy about this because the child's emotional security is key. Otherwise offer to do an activity together in the space where the child feels familiar.

When a parent most needs your help, she might be too overwhelmed to think through what she needs done. When you see a need, respond. Wash the dishes or tidy the kitchen. If you aren't sure she will want this task done - ask permission. It's not about creating a perfect house - it's about easing the load. Don't wait to be asked for help - offer to do something specific!

Perhaps you'd like to print these notes to give to someone who will be supporting a baby and toddler family.

Here's the link to the "Baby and Toddler Resources", where you can download these notes:

https://www.koemba.com/baby-and-toddler-resources/

A Note to Grandparents

This "Baby and Toddler On Board" book attempts to see life from the young child's perspective when baby joins the family. As a grandparent, I see the paradigm of parenting has changed since we raised our children. Now we realise we don't spoil children by responding to their cries for attention. Rather we are in danger of spoiling them if we ignore their genuine needs for connection and for affirmation, as wonderful, unique human beings.

It's time for our generation, as well as the parents of this era, to ask,

"What do children need to thrive, physically, cognitively, emotionally, socially and spiritually?"

APPENDIX 3

Help Val To Help Other Parents!

Thank you for reading this book.

If these three steps have given you helpful insights into how to mindfully parent a toddler or preschooler when baby joins the family, then please help me spread the message to parents around the world.

Please visit Amazon, or the platform where you purchased this book, or Goodreads, to write a review. This matters because most potential readers first judge a book by what others have to say.

If you have found
this book helpful,
please write a review,
so that other parents
discover it too.
Thank you. *Val*

&Toddler

Please share about this book by sending the link to any parent or caregiver you think will benefit from "Baby and Toddler On Board - Mindful Parenting When a New Baby Joins the Family":

https://www.koemba.com/baby-and-toddler-on-board-book/

If you mention the book on Social Media, please use the hashtag #BabyAndToddlerOnBoard

I greatly appreciate your support because you help other parents to know about my work as a resource that can create calmer, happier parenting.

APPENDIX 4

Other Books by Val Mullally

If you have enjoyed this book, I expect you'll also enjoy:

"BEHAVE - What To Do When Your Child Won't".available from http://www.Koemba.com/behave.

To be the parent you'd love to be, and respond to your child whilst setting limits where needed, isn't always easy. This book shares the three signposts to help parents when they are challenged with their child's behaviour. This book is most suitable for parents of children aged 2–10 years.

"This little gem is my go-to parenting book ..."

Orla Kelly

Here's what you can expect to learn while reading the "BEHAVE" book:

- Parenting tips and key insights about how to respond, rather than react, to your child, particularly at times when behaviour is challenging.

- Why punishment doesn't work; and how to discipline your child to meet your needs and theirs.

- Insightful information about what's happening inside our brains (and our children's) when we're stressed

- Practical parenting tools to create better connection, communication and cooperation which can lead to a happier, more cooperative home

STOP YELLING

9 Steps to Calmer Happier Parenting

Val Mullally

FREE bonus inside!

'Read it. Read it again. And again.'

Dr Patricia K Martin

As a mother-to-be, I wanted to ensure I had the tools to create a warm, respectful, fun and loving household I could be proud of. ... I ordered Val Mullally's "Stop Yelling - 9 Steps to Calmer Happier Parenting" with the hope her book would have tools that would support me to be the parent I want to be. The book was all I hoped it would be, I found it extremely empowering. The content was very easy to grasp and made a lot of sense.

Patricia Tiernan

Discover how to stop yelling at your kids and how to become a calmer, happier parent. This book is for you if you sometimes feel stressed and frustrated. Learn how to recalibrate your own parenting behaviour and move from upset to reconnection with your child. Sidestep the power struggle, to create win-win solutions for a happier, more co-operative family.

Buy this book now if you want to know how to stop yelling and start connecting with your children, whatever their age!

Stop Yelling – 9 Steps To Calmer, Happier Parenting available from https://www.koemba.com/the-9-steps-to-stop-the-yelling-book/

Here's what you can expect to learn while reading the "Stop Yelling" parenting book:

- 9 practical steps to become a calmer, happier parent
- how to ensure Frustration or Anxiety aren't in the driving seat
- how to put Frustration and Anxiety in the back seat and retake control
- how to recalibrate your own parenting behaviour
- how to chart your progress
- how to move from upset to reconnection to create a happier relationship with your child
- the importance of side-stepping the power struggle with your child
- how to create win-win solutions for a happier, more co-operative family
- how to quit the yelling habit once for all
- and much, much more

COMING SOON! - "Working With Under Sixes" by Val Mullally (Second edition)

A practical resource for child-minders, childcare workers, teachers and helpers in Early Education re how to nurture the holistic wellbeing of the young child.

APPENDIX 5

Resources and Supports

Join me in the Koemba community because then you'll gain insights, tips and strategies for happier parenting, and you'll also be amongst the first to know of new releases and gain from introductory offers and discounts.

Resources and Additional Supports

The Baby and Toddler resources can be accessed from https://www.koemba.com.

Get the support you need to be the parent you'd love to be.

✓ Sign up to the Koemba Parenting newsletter so you're one of the first to know of specials and new releases

✓ Discover Koemba Parenting online courses and workshops

✓ Get one-to-one Coaching support with Parenting Coach Val Mullally *

✓ Invite me to be your keynote speaker if you are looking for a warm and inspiring presenter for your seminar or conference

Of course, I'd also love you to connect with me on:

Twitter: @valmullally https://twitter.com/ValMullally

Facebook: https://www.facebook.com/Koemba

Pinterest: https://www.pinterest.ie/valmullally

* There is huge potential benefit in one-to-one, or couples, coaching – both online and face-to-face, which gives you your own personal space to work with me to create the family relationships you desire. I also offer group coaching, where parents can share from each other's experience and learning, as I offer coaching support. For more about parent coaching see https://www.koemba.com/coaching/

Why not ask to join the "Koemba Parenting Café" Facebook group, where we encourage one another to parent mindfully. Together we can help our families to:

- think more clearly

- connect more compassionately

- behave more response-ably

- and live more joyfully.

Why Val Mullally is your "go-to" Parenting Expert

Just as you choose with care any other professional person, because their personality and compassion matters as much as their expertise, I'm empathetic and understanding of the challenges of parenting because I've been in similar situations myself.

I'm not an author who is hidden away behind my laptop all day. I'm out in the real world and I'm confident you will find I:

- connect with you, whether it's on a one-to-one or in a masterclass or conference

- create a safe and enjoyable environment for you to discover your unique way forward as a family

- give clear insights and helpful practical parenting tools

- motivate and inspire you to be the parent you'd love to be

I'm passionate about supporting parents and professionals to create environments for children to thrive. You can read more about my background and experience working with parents and children on https://www.koemba.com/about/val-mullally/

My work, Koemba Parenting, is a unique blend of practical parent coaching tools with key insights from child development, relationship theory, emotional intelligence, coaching, NLP, attachment theory and neuroscience, which has grown from my experience as a teacher, principal, trainer, coach and, most importantly, from being a parent and grandparent!

For any other way I can support you, please contact me at: val@koemba.com or on the contact form on my website

https://www.koemba.com

APPENDIX 6

Recommended Reading

Crabb, Kimberly and Paine, April (2013) *The ABCs of Baby #2 - Surviving the Second Child One Letter at a Time* CreateSpace Independent Publishing Platform

Hilton Pearce (1992) *Magical Child - Rediscovering Nature's Plan for Our Children* PLUME - Penguin Books, USA

Gerhardt, Sue (2004) *Why Love Matters: how affection shapes a baby's brain* Rutledge, East Sussex

Gordon, Mary (2007) *Roots of Empathy: Changing The World One Child At A Time* The Experiment, New York

Juul, Jesper (1995) *Your Competent Child* Farrar, Straus & Giroux, New York

Louv, Richard (2008) *Last Child in the Woods: Saving Our Children from Nature-deficit Disorder* Atlantic Books, New York

Mullally, Val (2015) *BEHAVE: What To Do When Your Child Won't - The Three Pointers to Mindful Discipline* Koemba, Republic of Ireland

Mullally, Val (2018) *Stop Yelling - 9 Steps to Calmer, Happier Parenting* Koemba, Orla Kelly Publishers, Republic of Ireland

Nicholson, Barbara and Parker, Lysa (2009) *Attached At The Heart - 8 Proven Principles for Raising Connected and Compassionate Children* iUniverse, New York

Payne Bryson, Tina and Siegel, Daniel (2012) *The Whole Brain Child: 12 Proven Strategies To Nurture Your Child's Developing Brain* Constable & Robinson Ltd, London

Siegel, Daniel and Hartzell, Mary (2004) *Parenting from the Inside Out – How a Deeper Understanding Can Help You Raise Children Who Thrive* Jeremy P. Tarcher – Penguin, New York

Sunderland, Margot (2007) *The Science of Parenting* Dorling Kindersley, London

Acknowledgements

This book would never have been born without the input of many different people.

To every child who has influenced me - my own children, grandchildren, "adopted" grandchildren, family and friends' children, pupils, including those whose fleeting encounter left an impression, I thank you.

To my father, no longer in this world, and to my dear mother, you have always been great influences in my life.

To my husband Bill - you are the wind beneath my wings.

Thank you for the encouragement and support of my family, especially those in Denmark. This book was birthed because of your loving home, our discussions on child-rearing and about the creation of this book and your practical support.

Heartfelt appreciation to all who have supported in so many roles, including talented cover designer Anthony Mullally.

To Danish artist Anna Hasle www.annahasle.dk - your fun, yet sensitive illustrations capture the essence of this book. Thank you!

My appreciation to Irish artists Liam Lavery and Eithne Ring, for your generous help with image computerisation.

This book materialised through the commitment of the team who supported its writing and production. My appreciation to all who have edited, proof-read and given suggestions and feedback, with particular thanks to Ruth Dell (aka LBS) , Patricia Martin, Sharon Yarr, Jennifer McKeague, Maeve Murray, Cathy

O'Sullivan, Pavla Jurasek and Caz Koopman, founder of <u>Gentle Discipline (Ireland) Facebook group</u>. Special thanks to Jill Holtz, co-founder of <u>www.MyKidsTime.com</u>, who has generously written the Foreword, which so beautifully sets the tone of this book.

Thanks to all who assisted with publishing and marketing, especially <u>Orla Kelly</u> for her professional guidance, encouragement and publishing expertise, and also to talented, patient and supportive colleagues - webmaster Gabriel Merovingi and project coach Patricia Tiernan.

I am eternally grateful to loyal friend and awesome digital marketing strategist Marie Collins, who taught me so much about the best things in life, as well as how to use the internet to reach out to the global community. RIP, dearest friend.

My apologies to those whom I have not named, who have helped along the journey of this book's writing and publishing. To all who have encouraged me, especially in the moments I doubted, you know who you are - blessings and deep appreciation.

To all whose shoulders I have stood upon - authors, mentors, trainers, lecturers - you gave me a greater and a wider vision, thank you.

I also acknowledge everyone who supports my work, my blog, books, webinars, recordings, workshops, parenting courses and presentations.

You make it possible for me to continue to create new resources for parents and for caregivers working with children and families. Together we are creating a world in which children can experience the love and support that enables them to grow into their incredible uniqueness.

35247986R00121

Printed in Poland
by Amazon Fulfillment
Poland Sp. z o.o., Wrocław